T5-AXN-218

Applied

BC

TX 531 .O88 1987
Ott, Dana B.
  Applied food science laboratory
manual

Pergamon Titles
of Related Interest

Christie LIPID ANALYSIS, 2nd Edition
Birch/Cameron/Spencer FOOD SCIENCE, 3rd Edition
Gaman/Sherrington THE SCIENCE OF FOOD: AN INTRODUCTION
TO FOOD SCIENCE, NUTRITION AND MICROBIOLOGY, 2nd Edition
Gunstone/Norris LIPIDS IN FOODS: CHEMISTRY, BIOCHEMISTRY
AND TECHNOLOGY
Lawrie MEAT SCIENCE, 3rd Edition

Related Journals
(Free sample copies available upon request.)

NUTRITION RESEARCH
PROGRESS IN FOOD AND NUTRITION SCIENCE
FOOD AND CHEMICAL TOXICOLOGY
PROGRESS IN LIPID RESEARCH

Applied Food Science Laboratory Manual

Dana B. Ott, Ph.D.
Michigan State University

PERGAMON PRESS

New York ▪ Oxford ▪ Beijing ▪ Frankfurt ▪
São Paulo ▪ Sydney ▪ Tokyo ▪ Toronto

TX
531
.O88
1987

Pergamon Press Offices:

U.S.A.   Pergamon Press, Maxwell House, Fairview Park,
                               Elmsford, New York 10523, U.S.A.

U.K.   Pergamon Press, Headington Hill Hall,
                               Oxford OX3 0BW, England

PEOPLE'S REPUBLIC   Pergamon Press, Qianmen Hotel, Beijing,
OF CHINA   People's Republic of China

FEDERAL REPUBLIC   Pergamon Press, Hammerweg 6,
OF GERMANY   D-6242 Kronberg, Federal Republic of Germany

BRAZIL   Pergamon Editora, Rua Eça de Queiros, 346,
                               CEP 04011, São Paulo, Brazil

AUSTRALIA   Pergamon Press (Aust.) Pty., P.O. Box 544,
                               Potts Point, NSW 2011, Australia

JAPAN   Pergamon Press, 8th Floor, Matsuoka Central Building,
                               1-7-1 Nishishinjuku, Shinjuku-ku, Tokyo 160, Japan

CANADA   Pergamon Press Canada, Suite 104, 150 Consumers Road,
                               Willowdale, Ontario M2J 1P9, Canada

---

Copyright © 1987 Pergamon Books, Inc.

*All rights reserved. No part of this publication may be
reproduced, stored in a retrieval system or transmitted in
any form or by any means: electronic, electrostatic,
magnetic tape, mechanical, photocopying, recording or
otherwise, without permission in writing from the
publishers.*

First printing 1987

Library of Congress Cataloging in Publication Data

Ott, Dana B.
    Applied food science laboratory manual.

    1. Food--Analysis--Handbooks, manuals, etc.
2. Food--Composition--Handbooks, manuals, etc.
I. Title.
TX531.O88   1986   664'.007'8   86-9510
ISBN 0-08-034230-2 (pbk.)

Printed in the United States of America

Contents

Preface

The applied food science researcher wants to know what food constituents can do functionally in food systems or can be manipulated to do toward producing a useful food product that is acceptable to consumers. It is the purpose of this laboratory manual to teach basic food science concepts in an applied fashion utilizing the scientific method.

Experiments in this manual cover food chemistry concepts in the areas of carbohydrates, lipids, proteins, and plant pigments. The outstanding features of this text include the use of new food ingredients (i.e., fructose, aspartame, low-methoxy pectins, soy proteins) in the laboratory experiments; lists of equipment and supplies necessary to conduct the experiments and in the proper quantities for 18 students per laboratory section; thorough explanation of the theory of each experiment; clear citation of the objectives of each experiment; detailed explanation of procedures; objective and subjective test assessments; inclusion of data-recording sheets; study questions about the experiments that can be used for examinations; and provision of numerous references to enable the student to write scientific laboratory reports and/or design an independent laboratory project. Other features that are unique to this manual are Appendix A on equipment use instructions and chapter laboratory guidelines. There are enough experiments to fulfill either a one-quarter or a one-semester time period.

This text is intended for the serious upper-division food science, dietetic, and/or food and nutrition undergraduate who has a background in general and organic chemistry and is interested in the functional components of macronutrients and pigments in food systems. This text will be most useful for professors and students involved in university-level food science and experimental foods courses. The laboratory manual will also serve as a good reference for small food-product development laboratories in the food industry, foods and nutrition extension specialists, dietitians, and high-school science and home economics teachers.

Chapter 1

Introduction to Experimental Foods and Food Experimentation

Approximately 25 years ago the vast majority of scientists–technologists and production personnel in the food field did not receive formal training in food science as it has come to be recognized today.

At that time, very few colleges and universities offered a total curriculum leading to a degree in food science. Rather, many of these institutions were organized according to speciality along commodity lines. Thus, the food industry as well as government and academic institutions are largely made up of persons who received training in dairy, meat sciences, cereal chemistry, pomology, vegetable crops, horticulture, etc. Many others were trained as specialists in the basic and applied fields of chemistry, physics, microbiology, statistics and engineering. The more recent graduates have "food science"-labeled degrees.

WHAT IS EXPERIMENTAL FOODS?

It is the study of food science. However, food science is not easily defined. First, let's define the following terms.

Food
Any substance that is eaten or otherwise taken into the body to sustain physiological and psychological life, provide energy, or promote nutrition. We eat food for many reasons besides obtaining nutrients or nutrition. The substance of food is an array of known chemicals such as water, protein, carbohydrates, lipids, minerals and vitamins, pigments, and flavoring compounds, but its also an array of unknown chemicals that impart the sensory characteristics of color, flavor, texture, nutritive characteristics and other effects.

Processed Food
Preservation by canning and freezing that results in chemical but little structural change; extraction or dehydration (i.e., orange juice concentrate) that
produces significant structural and possibly major chemical changes; and
processes that involve extensive separation of foods into components (flour,
oil, sugar) or fabrication of new foods such as "chips" (made from moulded
rehydrated potato flakes) or cool whip, etc. that result in much structural
change that may have equally marked effects on the chemical composition of
foods (National Research Council, 1982).

Food Functionality
Any property of a food system or food ingredient, besides the nutritional
ones, that affects its utilization (Pour-El, 1981).

Food Science
The study of basic constituents of foods (carbohydrates, lipids, protein,
water) and the chemical, microbial, and physical actions and reactions that
cause nutritional, sensory, and other changes before, during, and after processing.

FOOD EXPERIMENTATION—THE SCIENTIFIC METHOD

History

In the early 17th century the era of modern science began, and with it came
a new way of thinking. Francis Bacon, Descartes, and Galileo rejected in-
spired authority and mystical thinking (i.e., taboos, magical properties of
food) as methods for learning in the natural world. These individuals concluded that nature had to be investigated impartially using sense, experience, and reason. They wanted a "surer method" of "finding out nature."
Their approach to learning developed into the scientific method.

Scientific Method

The scientific method is *basically a method for detecting error*; it does not
provide us with a series of truths, but it does enable us to detect what is
false. This is important to understand, for it is this method that has provided
us with our current knowledge of food science, nutrition, and other sciences. This method has the potential for resolving controversies over complex problems.

The scientific method is an "inductive method" (that is, using logical
reasoning from particular facts or individual cases to arrive at a general
conclusion). Science advances only by disproofs. Science proceeds at first by

negatives, and at last ends in affirmatives after exclusion has been exhausted.

However, disproof is a hard doctrine. We do not like to be wrong (i.e., if I have a hypothesis and you have another hypothesis, most likely one will be eliminated). The scientist seems to have no choice but to be either soft-headed or disputatious.

Preliminary information needed for the scientific method includes (a) a question, problem, speculation, or assumption; (b) a literature review, which is a gathering of information about the problem and the critical evaluation of this information; and (c) thinking about the question in light of the gathered information. Speculate how the problem can be solved and what the solution to the problem might be.

The scientific method includes the following sequence of steps.

1. *Develop a hypothesis.* A hypothesis is an assumption not proved by experiment or observation, a conclusion drawn before all of the facts are established. The hypothesis is more narrow than the original question and includes a predicted answer to be tested.

2. *Experimental plan.* The researcher tests methodically and logically the accuracy and reliability of the hypothesis while controlling as many variables as possible. Precision and accuracy are vital in carrying out the experiment so as to get a clean result.

3. *Evaluate the data.* Look at the data critically, answering the following questions: (a) Are the data reliable? (b) Did the experimental plan adequately test the question and answer it? Why or why not? (c) What are the conclusions? Also, the data need to be verified by other investigators in the field.

4. *Recycling procedure.* This is a step where the investigator makes subhypotheses or sequential hypotheses to refine the possibilities that remain about the original problem. You should come up with more questions at the end of the experiment than when you began the experiment. Hypotheses are abundant!

The scientific method is logical, is not difficult, and can be learned. Again, keep in mind that we are *disproving* our hypothesis most of the time! So don't be discouraged. We learn from our failures and mistakes!

SELECTED BIBLIOGRAPHY

National Research Council. 1982. *Diet, Nutrition and Cancer.* Assembly of Life Sciences. National Academy Press, Washington, D.C.

Pour-El, A. 1981. *Protein Functionality in Foods*, Chapter 1. ASC Symposium Series 147, American Chemical Council, Washington, D.C.

Chapter 2

Laboratory Guidelines/Responsibilities

LABORATORY RESPONSIBILITIES

1. To gain the most from the time spent in class and especially in the laboratory, do the assigned readings ahead of time; study the laboratory directions before coming to class and make sure that you understand what you are to do to complete the experiment successfully. Review instructions for the use of appropriate objective and subjective evaluation techniques.

2. Make certain that you understand why each problem and its variables are being studied. You should be familiar enough with the topic to anticipate the results of the experiment. Read and keep in mind the questions following the experiments. Be sure to answer the questions before proceeding to the next experiment. These questions may appear on examinations!

3. To derive the most learning value from your laboratory experience, ask yourself the following questions about each experiment:
   (a) Why is this experiment included?
   (b) What facts and principles are illustrated by the results?
   (c) Do the results obtained agree with the literature?
   (d) To what other food systems does information from this experiment apply?
   (e) What other experiments or variables might have been included to provide additional information?
   (f) How can knowledge from this experiment be applied to my career goals?
   (g) What other experiments or variables might have been included to help meet the U.S. Dietary Guidelines?

4. Before beginning your work on an experiment gather together the equip-

ment and materials you need to carry it through to completion. The lack of ingredients or equipment at the right time may lead to poor results or failure. Practice good management principles. Arrange equipment and supplies for maximum efficiency.

5. Professional conduct is to be maintained throughout the laboratory sessions.
6. Keep conversation to a low roar! It is difficult to concentrate when surrounded by loud chatter.
7. All students are responsible for the condition of the laboratory at the end of the lab session.

PROFESSIONAL APPEARANCE

1. Each student will be required to wear a clean white laboratory coat or smock. Students will not be allowed to work in the lab without the appropriate attire. Each student is responsible for keeping garments clean. A clean uniform or laboratory coat is desirable for sanitation in the laboratory as well as for protection of regular clothing.
2. Appropriate shoes must be worn in the lab. Shoes must be low heeled with closed toes.
3. Hair must be contained. If long, hair must be up out of the way or clipped back.
4. Good personal hygiene must be followed.

LABORATORY—GENERAL RULES

1. Before beginning the experiment:
   (a) Read the experiment carefully.
   (b) Decide which individuals will manage a specific segment of the experiment.
   (c) Wash hands.
   (d) Assemble necessary utensils and supplies.
   (e) Read labels accurately, weigh and measure accurately, use open containers first, discard or clean empty containers. Take only the amount needed to your unit.
   (f) Carry supplies to and from the supply table on trays.
   (g) Have all materials measured and ready to use before beginning the experiment.
2. During the preparation of the experiment:
   (a) Keep your lab bench in order. Clean up spills. Clean up as you go along (this may include utensils no longer needed); reuse equipment when possible; scrape, rinse or soak utensils before washing. To im-

prove the ease of working and the general appearance of the room, clutter should be avoided in the laboratory.

(b) Place soiled utensils, such as knives, forks, spoons, etc., on a tray.

(c) Use a tasting spoon for sampling food; keep it reserved strictly for individual use.

(d) Keep jars and cans covered on the supply table.

(e) After using equipment and/or supplies, be sure they are properly cleaned and prepared for storage and/or future use.

(f) Return equipment and/or supplies to your own lab space or other storage places from which obtained as soon as possible.

(g) Put all wastes in garbage cans or in the garbage disposal. Never "force" large amounts of food waste into the disposal; instead "feed" the food waste down the drain continuously a small amount at a time (while the water is running and the disposal is operating). Do not allow glass, metal, crockery, wood, straw, string, paper, cloth, celery, bones, pineapple, banana peel, corn husks or cobs, artichoke leaves, pea and lima bean pods, and rubber bands to enter the drain. If this occurs, stop the disposal and remove these items.

(h) Check with the instructor regarding equipment and glassware breakage and replacement. The instructor will give directions for disposing of tin cans, broken dishes, oil, etc.

3. Clean-up:

(a) Assemble soiled dishes and utensils.

(b) Wipe greasy dishes and utensils with paper towels.

(c) Soak dishes that contain sugary items in hot water.

(d) Soak dishes or utensils that contain egg, milk, and starchy items in cold water.

(e) Half-fill sink or dishpan with hot detergent suds for washing dishes.

(f) Scour equipment as needed with cleaning powder or steel wool.

(g) Rinse with boiling water.

(h) Clean work surfaces thoroughly (if used).

(i) Clean sink thoroughly; clean strainer (if used).

(j) Clean range top, burners, oven, and broiler (if used).

4. At the close of the laboratory:

(a) Return all utensils and dishes to proper places in the laboratory.

(b) Wring dishcloths and towels as dry as possible. Place in the appropriate location in the laboratory.

(c) Close all doors and drawers.

(d) Make sure all ovens, stove tops, and equipment are turned off.

(e) Return special equipment and dishes to proper areas or to the supply cart.

(f) Place waste paper and wrapped garbage in containers provided.

(g) Sweep floor in unit area if glass is broken, sugar spilled, and/or rapeseeds are spilled, etc.
(h) Cover perishables and refrigerate.
(i) Align tables and chairs neatly at end of class.

Chapter 3

Experiment: Accuracy and Precision of Measurements: Metric System vs. English System

THEORY

Carefully controlled experiments are necessary if the results are to be meaningful and, in the case of more extensive research studies, worthy of publication. The experiments in this laboratory manual are designed to be controlled experiments; in other words, one factor is varied while all other conditions that might affect the results are controlled as much as possible. If more than one factor is altered, it is difficult to determine the cause of any changes that might be observed in the quality of the products. Even in the most carefully planned experiment, unexpected variables may arise. Temperature and humidity of the laboratory are difficult to control but may influence the results of an experiment. Faulty measurements, misinterpretation of instructions, and variation in individual techniques are other possible unexpected variables that should be considered.

Household measuring devices were designed for quick and easy use with enough accuracy and precision for home use. The American Standards Association, in accordance with the recommendations of the American Home Economics Association (AHEA), established standards for the capacity of household measuring devices. These utensils were volume-measuring devices. A tolerance of 5% has been accepted for these measuring utensils. Thus, the 1 cup measure with a standard capacity of 236.6 ml could actually have a capacity of 224.8–248.4 ml. The 250 ml measure to be adopted for use in the United States will have to have a capacity within the range of 237.5–262.5 ml.

Household measuring utensils such as a customary 1 cup liquid measure lack precision because their diameters at the point of measurement are larger than the diameters of more precise measuring devices, such as 100 ml pipets, 100 ml burets, or 100 ml graduated cylinders. A difference of a few drops in the volume of the liquid measure shows very clearly in a pipet or buret, somewhat less clearly in a graduated cylinder, and far less clearly in a household measuring device. Therefore, a measuring utensil no larger than required is selected when possible. Errors in measuring food by volume may be caused by the manner in which measuring devices are used. Liquid measurements should be read at eye level and the position of the bottom of the meniscus noted. The way in which a food is handled for measurement will influence the precision of measurement. The weight of a measured cup of food may reflect variations in the food itself as well as in the way in which it is measured.

For experimental work, the amount of each ingredient in a formula is usually controlled by weighing, except that liquids sometimes are measured in a graduated cylinder.

OBJECTIVES

1. To contrast the accuracy of home measuring equipment with the use of the top-loading balance.
2. To compare the accuracy of volume measurements in a home measuring cup to the use of graduated cylinders.
3. To understand the difference between accuracy and precision.
4. To understand and cite reasons why the metric system is used in experimental foods research.

MATERIALS

All-purpose white flour   10 lb

PROCEDURE

Each person will do the following.

1. First, read the instructions on how to use the top-loading balances (see Appendix A).
2. Next, weigh and record the weight (see data sheet) of the 1/4 cup measuring utensil that will be used to measure 1/4 cup of all-purpose flour by the following methods.
   (a) All-purpose flour sifted once and then lightly spooned into the appropriate measuring cup. Measurement is completed by leveling with the

straight edge of a metal spatula. Weigh and record weight of sample. Repeat this procedure.
(b) All-purpose flour (unsifted) spooned into the appropriate measuring cup and leveled with the straight edge of a metal spatula. Weigh and record weight of sample. Repeat this procedure.
(c) All-purpose flour sifted directly into the appropriate measuring cup and leveled with the straight edge of a metal spatula. Weigh and record weight of sample. Repeat this procedure.
(d) Fill a glass measuring cup with water to the $1/2$ cup mark. Pour the water into a 250 ml or 300 ml graduated cylinder. Record the volume. Repeat this procedure two more times.

STUDY QUESTIONS

1. Which is more accurate: using a balance or using a home measuring device? Why?
2. Is it necessary to sift all-purpose flour before weighing? Why?
3. Compare the actual volumes of water in the graduated cylinder with the expected volumes. Why were there discrepancies?
4. Distinguish between precision and accuracy.
5. Why should ingredients be weighed rather than measured by volume for experimental foods research?

SELECTED BIBLIOGRAPHY

American Standards Association. 1949. *American Standard Dimensions, Tolerances, and Terminology for Home Cooking and Baking Utensils*, Z61.1. Author, New York.
Arlin, M. L., Nielson, M. M., and Hall, F. T. 1964. The effect of different methods of flour measurement on the quality of plain two-egg cakes. *J. Home Econ.* 56:399.
Charley, H. 1982. *Food Science*, chapter 2. John Wiley & Sons, New York.
Grewe, E. 1932. Variation in the weight of a given volume of different flours. I. Normal variations. *Cereal Chem.* 9:311.
Grewe, E. 1932. Variation in the weight of a given volume of different flours. II. The result of the use of different wheats. *Cereal Chem.* 9:531.
Grewe, E. 1932. Variation in the weight of a given volume of different flours. III. Causes for variation, milling, blending, handling, and time of storage. *Cereal Chem.* 9:628.
Miller, B. S. and Trimbo, H. B. 1972. Use of metric measurements in food preparation. *J. Home Econ.* 64(2):20.

DATA SHEET

ACCURACY AND PRECISION OF MEASUREMENTS: METRIC SYSTEM VS. ENGLISH SYSTEM

NAME   _____

DATE   _____

1. Weight of container   _____ g

2. Weight of all-purpose flour, sifted*

	weight no. 1	_____ g
weight no. 2	_____ g
average weight	_____ g

3. Weight of all-purpose flour, unsifted*

weight no. 1	_____ g
weight no. 2	_____ g
average weight	_____ g

4. Weight of all-purpose flour, sifted into cup*

weight no. 1	_____ g
weight no. 2	_____ g
average weight	_____ g

5. Volume of 1/2 cup water

volume no. 1	_____ ml
volume no. 2	_____ ml
volume no. 3	_____ ml
average volume	_____ ml

*Remember to subtract the weight of the container from the same container filled with flour to obtain the weight of the flour.

Chapter 4

Experiment: Sensory Assessment of Food Quality

THEORY

The production of finished foods, either by the farmer or by the food processor, implies that the consumer will accept these products and pay the requisite price, i.e., that the product has a certain quality. It is easier to recognize quality than to define it. Quality is obviously some sort of mental summation of the physical and chemical properties of the food. Many sensory factors are involved. Chemical and physical tests, although they give much useful information and frequently can be correlated with quality, must be supplemented with sensory tests.

Sensory evaluation of food or evaluation of food quality by a panel of judges is essential to most food experiments because it answers the important questions of how a food looks, smells, feels, and tastes. The Sensory Division of the Institute of Food Technologists (1981) defines sensory evaluation as "a scientific discipline used to evoke, measure, analyze, and interpret reactions to those characteristics of foods and materials as they are perceived by the senses of sight, taste, touch, and hearing."

The answers to the questions posed in sensory evaluation may seem easy, but they are actually difficult because the answers depend on human judgment, which is individual and not always consistent. Many types of sensory tests are used in food research. Panelists may be asked to discriminate among samples, describe or score the quality of a product, rate the acceptability of a product, or describe their preference for a product. The test selected will depend on the objectives of the investigation. Sensory methods frequently are supplemented with chemical and physical methods of evaluation of food quality.

OBJECTIVES

1. To become familiar with a selection of sensory tests available for evaluating food products.
2. To compare the reliability and function of representative sensory tests.
3. To demonstrate knowledge of the advantages and disadvantages of various sensory measurements.

MATERIALS

paper souffle cups—4 oz size	100
paper cups—4 oz size	200
peach slices, canned, brand 1	$1^1/_2$ qt
peach slices, canned, brand 2	$1^1/_2$ qt
Pepsi, diet	2 L
Coke, diet	2 L
grapefruit juice, canned, unsweetened	2 L
angel food cake	1 small
white sugar (sucrose), granulated	2 cups

PROCEDURE

Difference Tests (Discriminative)

Duo–trio Test

Two brands of peach slices have been provided for this test. Using the brand present in the largest quantity, prepare one sample (about 25 g) of the peaches in 4 oz soufflé cups, and label it as R (reference). Prepare one additional sample of this brand, assign it a number of 166 or 466. Prepare another sample using the second brand of peaches and assign it the remaining random number. Inform the judge that the R sample is the reference sample. The panelist is asked to indicate which of the other two samples *differs* from the control. After scoring has been completed by your lab partner on the duo–trio test form (see data sheet), we will calculate the percentage of correct responses of the entire class.

Triangle Test

Pepsi and Coke have been provided for this test. Using small paper cups, prepare two samples of Pepsi or Coke (your choice), approximately 60 ml each. These two samples are the *same brand*. Label one sample by one random number (use 133, 400, or 512) and the remaining sample by a second random number. Prepare another sample, using the other brand of drink, and label with the remaining random number. Your lab partner is to taste the products and *indicate* the *odd sample*. After scoring has been completed by your lab partner on the appropriate form, we will calculate the percentage of correct responses of the entire class.

Quality Tests (Descriptive)

Ranking Tests
Grapefruit juice has been provided for this test. To produce increased sweetness in three 120 ml samples, add 2.5 g, 5 g, and 10 g, respectively, of sucrose to the 120 ml of juice samples. Using the random numbers 344, 977, 277, and 688, assign a number to each of the sweetened variables and to a fourth unsweetened one (120 ml). Record these identifications on the appropriate form. Your partner is to rank this series of samples in *increasing order of sweetness*. After scoring has been completed by your lab partner, we will calculate the percentage of correct responses in the class for each variable.

Acceptance/Preference Tests

Hedonic Tests
Angel food cake has been provided for use with the hedonic scale, ranging from like extremely to dislike extremely. Each lab partner will taste the cake samples and then record their response on the provided form. As a class, we will calculate the mean score for the test sample.

STUDY QUESTIONS

1. What are the advantages and disadvantages of using sensory tests in the evaluation of food products?
2. What are the advantages and disadvantages of the sensory tests demonstrated in this experiment?
3. Define the following terms: flavor, taste, odor, texture, tender, tough, sensory evaluation.
4. Describe the purpose of
   (a) discrimination tests,
   (b) descriptive tests,
   (c) acceptance/preference tests.
5. What are some variables to keep in mind when interpreting results?

SELECTED BIBLIOGRAPHY

Amerine, M. A., Pangborn, R. M., and Roessler, E. B. 1965. *Principles of Sensory Evaluation of Foods*, chapter 6. Academic Press, New York.
Birch, G. G., Brennan, J. G., and Parker, K. J. 1977. *Sensory Properties of Foods*.

The King's Library

Applied Science Publishers, London.

Brandt, F. I. and Arnold, R. G. 1977. Sensory tests used in food product development. *Food Prod. Dev.* 11(8):56.

Campbell, A. M., Penfield, M. P., and Griswold, R. M. 1979. *The Experimental Study of Food*, chapter 15. Houghton Mifflin, Boston, MA.

Charley, H. 1982. *Food Science*, chapter 1. John Wiley & Sons, New York.

Genser, M. V., Moskowitz, H. R., Solms, J., and Roth, J. J. 1977. *Sensory Response to Food: A Sensory Workshop*. Forster Verlag AG, Zurich.

Hirsh, N. L. 1970. Getting fullest value from sensory testing. Part I: Use and misuse of testing methods. *Food Prod. Dev.* 8(10):33.

Hirsh, N. L. 1975. Getting fullest value from sensory testing. Part III: Use and misuse of test panels. *Food Prod. Dev.* 9(2):78.

Institute of Food Technologists. 1981. Sensory evaluation guide for testing food and beverage products. *Food Technol.* 35(11):50.

Kramer, A. and Szczesniak, A. S. 1973. *Texture Measurements of Foods*, chapter 3. D. Reidel, Boston, MA.

Pangborn, R. M. 1980. Sensory science today. *Cereal Foods World* 25:637.

Paul, P. C. and Palmer, H. H. 1972. *Food Theory and Applications*, chapter 15. John Wiley & Sons, New York.

Powers, J. J. and Moskowitz, H. R. 1976. Correlating sensory objective measurements — new method for answering old problems. *STP* 594, American Society for Testing and Materials, Philadelphia, PA.

Prell, P. A. 1976. Preparation of reports and manuscripts which include sensory evaluation data. *Food Technol.* 30(11):40.

Stahl, W. H. and Einstein, M.A. 1973. Sensory testing methods. In *Encyclopedia of Industrial Chemical Analysis*, Vol. 17, p. 608. John Wiley & Sons, New York.

Szczesniak, A. S., Brandt, M. A., and Friedman, H. H. 1963. Development of standard rating scales for mechanical parameters of texture and correlation between the objective and sensory methods of texture evaluation. *J. Food Sci.* 28:397.

The King's Library

DATA SHEET
SENSORY ASSESSMENT OF FOOD QUALITY

NAME _____

DATE _____

PRODUCT _____canned peach slices_____

Duo–Trio Test

Directions: Observe and taste the reference slice of a peach labeled R. Taste the other samples and check the code number of the sample which *differs* from the reference sample.

Code Number	Differs from (R)
466	_____
166	_____

PRODUCT _____soft drinks_____

Triangle Test

Directions: Two of the samples are identical, the other is different. Please indicate the *odd* sample.

Code Number	Odd Sample (indicate by X)
133	_____
400	_____
512	_____

Describe the difference in the samples, if possible!

DATA SHEET
SENSORY ASSESSMENT OF FOOD QUALITY

NAME _____

DATE _____

PRODUCT _____ grapefruit juice _____

Ranking Test

Directions: Please rank the grapefruit juice samples in order of *increasing intensity* of sweetness.

Sample codes: 344   977   277   688

	Code Number
Least intense	_____
	_____
	_____
Most intense	_____

PRODUCT _____ angel food cake _____

Hedonic Scale Test

Directions: On the following scale check the comment that best describes how much you *like* or *dislike* the sample you have tasted. Keep in mind that you are the judge. You are the only one who can tell what you like. Nobody knows whether this food should be considered good, bad, or indifferent. An honest expression of your personal feeling will help us to decide.

_____ Like extremely (7)
_____ Like moderately (6)
_____ Like slightly (5)
_____ Neither like/dislike (4)
_____ Dislike slightly (3)
_____ Dislike moderately (2)
_____ Dislike extremely (1)

Comments:

Chapter 5

Experiment: Objective Assessment of Food Quality

THEORY

Food quality testing methods that do not depend on the observations of an individual (human senses) and can be repeated by using an instrument or a standard procedure are described as objective methods. Objective methods include a wide variety of physical and chemical tests, such as the following.

Chemical Methods

Chemical methods include the determination of the nutritive value of foods before and after cooking, as well as of constituents that affect the palatability of the food, such as peroxides in fats.

Physiochemical Methods

Certain physiochemical determinations are important in food analysis. Of these, probably the one most frequently used is hydrogen ion concentration, or pH. Measurement with a refractometer of refractive index, the angle to which light is bent by certain substances, is useful in finding the sugar concentration of syrups and the degree of hydrogenation of fats. The determination with a polariscope of the rotation of plane-polarized light by sugar solutions offers a method for their quantitative analysis.

Microscopic Examination

Some properties of foods depend on the structure or physical arrangement of their components. Microscopic examination of foods such as mayonnaise, whipped cream, fondant, and cake batter may yield valuable information.

18

Fiber diameters and sarcomere lengths of meat samples can be measured easily with the ocular measuring device of a microscope.

Physical Properties

Some physical properties, such as temperature, length, or the amount of liquid drained from the food on standing, are simple and used frequently. Others, on which attention will be focused, are of special interest because they are related to the results of sensory tests. These tests are made with special instruments or with improvised devices.

Many objective tests used to assess food textures are empirical in nature. Although the information provided may not be of a fundamental, rheological character, it is a valid and meaningful index to the texture of a food. Measuring the force needed to break crisp pastry or cookies with a shortometer or the resistance of a molded gelatin or of cooked vegetables to penetration by the needle or cone of a penetrometer are examples of empirical tests for food texture.

One aspect of meat tenderness may be assessed by a penetrometer, but a shearing device is more commonly used. A hydraulic press is sometimes used to measure the expressible liquid from cooked meats. A hand-held pressure tester is used to determine the optimum stage of maturity for picking such fruits as pears. A line-spread test may be used to measure differences in the consistency of batters, puddings, and sauces. A compressimeter is used to measure the firmness or staleness of bread. A sophisticated instrument, the Instron Universal Testing Machine, is now widely used to measure a number of aspects of the textural properties of foods.

The advantages of these tests are numerous. They may offer a permanent record of results and invite confidence because they are reproducible and less subject to error than sensory methods of evaluation. Selection of objective tests should involve care. The selected method should give results that are in agreement with the sensory evaluation results. If the two methods do not correlate, they may not be measuring the same component of quality and hence the chemical or physical method may not be useful for the study.

OBJECTIVES

1. To become familiar with and to demonstrate the use of the objective testing instruments that are available in the laboratory for evaluating food products.
2. To demonstrate knowledge of the advantages, disadvantages, and types of food samples required for specific objective instruments.
3. To understand the sensory attributes of the food product that can possibly be correlated with the use of specific objective instruments.

MATERIALS

muffins	1 doz
short bread cookies	2 doz
flank steak	1 1/2 lb
custard, canned	2 qt
skewers	18
rulers	18

PROCEDURES

Each person will become familiar with the use of each objective test measurement (see Appendix A for instrument diagrams and instructions). The instruments to be used in this experiment are as follows.

Objective Tests

Volumeter
Food to be measured: muffins. Find the volume of the product by subtracting the volume of rapeseed required to fill the empty container from the measured volume of rapeseed required to fill the container that holds the food product for which the volume is being measured. After the volume of the product has been determined, divide the volume of the product by the weight of the product. Report as specific volume in units of cubic centimeters per gram.

Bailey Shortometer
Food to be measured: short bread cookies. Record the force required to break the product.

Warner–Bratzler Shear
Food to be measured: flank steak. Record the force required to shear the sample.

Carver Press
Food to be measured: flank steak. Record the percentage of press fluid.

Penetrometer
Food to be measured: custard. Record the millimeters required to penetrate the sample for 30 sec using the aluminum cone.

Line Spread Test
Food to be measured: custard. Allow the custard to spread 1 min before taking readings. Average the four readings taken. Calculate the percent sag.

Percent Sag Test

Percent sag is a convenient test to measure gel strength. Measure the height of the gel in its container by inserting a skewer and checking the distance on the measure. Loosen the gel from the container and invert onto a glass plate. Measure the height. Percent sag is calculated as

$$\text{Percent sag} = \frac{\text{height in container} - \text{height out of container}}{\text{height in container}} \times 100$$

STUDY QUESTIONS

1. What are the advantages and disadvantages of using objective tests to measure food quality attributes?
2. What specific food quality attributes do the instruments used in this experiment measure?
3. What general types of food items can specific instruments be used upon?
4. What does percent sag indicate?
5. Define the following terms: rheology, viscosity, elasticity, shearability, objective methods.
6. Why was the specific volume of the muffin determined?

SELECTED BIBLIOGRAPHY

Babb, A. T. S. 1965. A recording instrument for the rapid evaluation of the compressibility of bakery goods. *J. Sci. Food Agric.* **16**:670.

Bourne, M. C. 1965. Studies on punch testing of apples. *Food Technol.* **19**:413.

Bouton, P. E. and Harris, P. W. 1972. The effects of cooking temperature and time on some mechanical properties of meat. *J. Food Sci.* **37**:140.

Bouton, P. E., Ford, A. L., Harris, P. V., and Ratcliff, D. 1975. A research note — objective assessment of meat juiciness. *J. Food Sci.* **40**:884.

Breene, W. M. 1975. Problems in instrumental analysis of texture in foods. *J. Texture Studies* **6**:53.

Campbell, A. M., Penfield, M .P., and Griswold, R. M. 1979. *The Experimental Study of Food*, chapter 15. Hougton Mifflin, Boston, MA.

Cathcart, W. H. and Cole, L. C. 1938. Wide-range volume-measuring apparatus for bread. *Cereal Chem.* **15**:69.

Charley, H. 1982. *Food Science*, chapter 1. John Wiley & Sons, New York.

Clydesdale, F. M. 1972. Measuring the color of foods. *Food Technol.* **26**(7):45.

Clydesdale, F. M. 1976. Instrumental techniques for color measurement of foods. *Food Technol.* **30**(10):52.

Friedman, H. H., Whitney, J. E., and Szczesniak, A. S. 1963. The texturometer — a new instrument for objective texture measurement. *J. Food Sci.* **28**:390.

Funk, K., Zabik, M. E., and Elgidaily, D. A. 1969. Objective measurements for baked products. *J. Home Econ.* **61**:119.

Grawemeyer, E. A. and Pfund, M. C. 1943. Line-spread as an objective test for consistency. *Food Res.* **8**:105.

Kastner, C. L. and Henrickson, R. L. 1969. Providing uniform meat cores for mechanical stress force measurement. *J. Food Sci.* **34**:603.

Kramer, A. and Szczesniak, A. S. 1973. *Texture Measurements of Foods*, chapter 3. D. Reidel, Boston, MA.

McWilliams, M. 1981. *Experimental Foods Laboratory Manual*, 2nd ed., chapter 1. Plycon Press, Redondo Beach, CA.

Noble, A. C. 1975. Instrumental analysis of the sensory properties of food. *Food Technol.* **29**(12):56.

Paul, P. C. and Palmer, H. H. 1972. *Food Theory and Applications*, chapter 15. John Wiley & Sons, New York.

Shuey, W. C. 1975. Practical instruments for rheological measurements of wheat products. *Cereal Chem.* **52**(311):42r.

Stinson, C. G. and Huck, M. B. 1969. A comparison of four methods for pastry tenderness evaluation. *J. Food Sci.* **34**:537.

Szczesniak, A. S. 1963. Classification of textural characteristics. *J. Food Sci.* **28**:385.

Szczesniak, A. S. 1963. Objective measurements of food texture. *J. Food Sci.* **28**:410.

Szczesniak, A. S. 1972. Texture measurement. *Food Technol.* **20**:1292–1296.

Szczesniak, A. S. 1973. Indirect methods of objective texture measurements. In *Texture Measurements of Food*, Kramer, A. and Szczesniak, A. S. (Eds.). Reidel, Boston, MA.

Szczesniak, A. S. 1975. General Foods texture profile revisited — Ten year perspective. *J. Texture Studies* **6**:5.

Szczesniak, A. S. 1977. An overview of recent advances in food texture research. *Food Technol.* **31**(4):71.

Szczesniak, A. S., Brandt, M. A., and Friedman, H. H. 1963. Development of standard rating scales for mechanical parameters of texture and correlation between the objective and the sensory methods of texture evaluation. *J. Food Sci.* **28**:397.

Szczesniak, A. S., Humbaugh, P. R., and Block, H. W. 1970. Behavior of different foods in the standard shear compression cell of the shear press and the effect of sample weight on peak area and maximum force. *J. Texture Studies* **1**:356.

Szczesniak, A. S. and Torgenson, K. W. 1965. Methods of meat texture measurement viewed from the background of factors affecting tenderness. *Adv. Food Res.* **14**:33.

DATA SHEET
OBJECTIVE ASSESSMENT OF FOOD QUALITY

NAME _____

DATE _____

INSTRUMENT	DATA
Volumeter	volume = _____ cm^3
	specific volume = _____ cm^3/g
Bailey shortometer	force = _____ oz
Warner–Bratzler shear	force = _____ 1b/mm diam. sample
Carver press	% press fluid = _____
Penetrometer	penetration = _____ mm/30 sec
Line-spread test	average of four values = _____ cm/min
Percent sag test	% sag = _____

Chapter 6

Experiment:
Carbohydrate Crystallization

THEORY

Crystallization is dependent upon a supersaturated solution and results in a crystal lattice formation. Thus, there is a change in physical state—from a liquid state to a solid state. In a crystalline candy, many small carbohydrate crystals are suspended in a small amount of concentrated sugar solution.

Carbohydrate crystallization is influenced by production methods as well as ingredients in the product formulation.

Production Methods

Concentration
As water is boiled out of an aqueous solution, the solution becomes increasingly concentrated. The carbohydrate concentration achieved during boiling determines the amount of sugar that ultimately will crystallize and, therefore, the firmness of the product. Underconcentration results in a soft product, whereas overconcentration results in a hard product. If the concentration step is not conducted properly, succeeding steps cannot compensate.

Rate of Heating
The rate of heating is not critical unless an acidic ingredient is present, but it should be similar for all samples being compared in an experiment. If an acidic ingredient, such as tartaric acid (cream of tartar) is present, the rate of heating is extremely important because inversion of sucrose occurs. Inversion, which occurs during heating, affects the ability of the sucrose to crystallize in a later step. The extent of inversion depends on the concentration of the acidic ingredient and on the length of time that it has an opportunity to act.

24

Cooling
The solution should be undisturbed during cooling; otherwise, premature crystallization is likely to occur, resulting in a grainy product. The extent of supersaturation, which is important to the crystallization process, increases as cooling proceeds.

Beating
Crystallization is initiated when beating is begun. If beating is begun when the solution is quite hot, crystallization is rapid, and the product is grainy. If beating is delayed until the solution has cooled to room temperature, beating is difficult, crystallization is slow, and the product is smooth. The preceding two statements at first seem to contradict theory, because if the extent of supersaturation increases with cooling, one might expect crystallization to occur more readily in the cooler, more highly supersaturated solution. However, viscosity is involved. In crystallization, the molecules align themselves into definite patterns to form crystals, each containing many oriented molecules. The molecules can move into their proper positions more readily in a syrup of relatively low viscosity than in one of high viscosity. A moderate extent of cooling provides for adequate development of supersaturation, in a properly concentrated syrup, without too great a viscosity.

Once initiated by beating, crystallization continues spontaneously. However, beating is continued for the purpose of keeping the crystals small and the product smooth. If crystallization occurs very rapidly, as in a hot syrup, even vigorous beating may not result in a smooth product. On the other hand, cooling to room temperature would be rather wasteful of time and energy. A temperature of 40–50°C (105–122°F) for the beginning of beating favors both reasonably rapid crystallization and the formation of small crystals.

Ingredients

Crystalline products may have numerous ingredients in their formulations which may have either chemical or physical effects on crystallization.

Chemical Effects
Tartaric acid causes sucrose inversion, which results in retardation of crystallization. Crystallization is less rapid from a solution of mixed sugars than from a solution of a single sugar. The different kinds of molecules must sort themselves out during crystal formation. Crystals tend to be small because of the slower crystallization.

Physical Effects
Lipids are an example of substances that have a physical effect on crystallization. Lipids tend to be absorbed on surfaces of crystals as they form and thus interfere with the growth of large crystals. Proteins, such as that in milk

solids, act similarly to lipids. These substances exert their effect during the beating stage. Addition of corn syrup or honey also retards crystallization and thus promotes smoothness. With either of these substances, the effect is similar to that of tartaric acid.

OBJECTIVES

1. To understand the interrelationship between the boiling temperature of a sugar solution and the firmness of the resulting crystalline product.
2. To identify and discuss the procedural and ingredient factors influencing the firmness and texture of a crystalline product.
3. To define a supersaturated solution, how it is produced, and to discuss its significance in making high-quality crystalline candy products.
4. To understand how the rate of heating influences the firmness and texture of crystalline candies.
5. To understand the mechanisms by which the different crystallization agents exert their interfering effects.

MATERIALS

sucrose, white granulated	7 lb
fructose, granulated	2 lb
chocolate, unsweetened	14 sq
cocoa powder, unsweetened	$3/4$ cups
milk, evaporated	9 cups
corn syrup, light	4 tb
water	5 cups
butter	1 lb
cream of tartar (tartaric acid)	2 oz
laboratory thermometers	18
penetrometer with needle attachment	1
saucepans, 1 qt	18
waxed paper	1 roll
paper plates, small (6 in.)	3 doz

PRODUCT FORMULATION (BASIC)

sucrose, granulated	200 g
milk, evaporated	160 ml
chocolate, unsweetened	28 g
butter	14 g
corn syrup, light	0.7 g

PROCEDURES (BASIC)

1. Weigh or measure all of the ingredients using top-loading balances and/ or graduated cylinders.
2. Calibrate thermometers. Adjust procedure temperatures accordingly.
3. Place sugar, corn syrup, evaporated milk, and chocolate in a 1 qt sauce pan.
4. Attach a thermometer to the side of the saucepan and immerse the bulb in the candy mixture, but do not allow the bulb to touch the side or bottom of the pan.
5. Heat slowly at first while stirring with a wooden spoon.
6. After the chocolate has melted, gradually increase the rate of heating to boil the mixture rapidly while stirring constantly.
7. Boil to a final temperature of 112°C (234°F).
8. Remove the mixture from the heat, but leave the thermometer in the candy so that it can be read. Avoid stirring and unnecessary movement of the hot mixture and the thermometer.
9. Immediately add the butter without stirring.
10. Let the mixture cool undisturbed until the temperature is 50°C (122°F).
11. Next, beat the mixture vigorously with a wooden spoon until the fudge lightens in color, thickens, and appears to be ready to set. This may take up to 20 min for some formulations.
12. Place the product on waxed paper and shape into a rectangle (if possible) 1 in. thick. Wrap in waxed paper; label the product with lab section number, date, lab partner names, and variable(s) studied.
13. Refrigerate until the next laboratory session when the crystalline products will be evaluated.

VARIABLES

1. Ingredients (for all ingredients the basic procedures are to be followed)
    (a) **Control.** Prepare the basic product formulation following the basic procedures.
    (b) **Water substitution** (100%). Prepare the basic product formulation but substitute 160 ml water in place of the 160 ml evaporated milk.
    (c) **Water/milk substitution** (50%). Prepare the basic product formulation but substitute 80 ml water plus 80 ml evaporated milk instead of the 160 ml evaporated milk.
    (d) **Tartaric acid (cream of tartar).** Prepare the basic product formulation but add 0.5 g tartaric acid before the mixture is heat treated.
    (e) **Fructose.** Prepare the basic product formulation but substitute 200 g granulated fructose instead of the 200 g granulated sucrose.
    (f) **Fructose/sucrose substitution** (50%). Prepare the basic product formulation but substitute 100 g granulated fructose plus 100 g granulated sucrose instead of the 200 g granulated sucrose.

(g) *Cocoa/butter*. Prepare the basic product formulation but substitute 22.5 g cocoa plus 7 g butter instead of the 28 g unsweetened chocolate. This additional butter is added in the same step as the cocoa ingredient.

2. Ingredients/final temperature (for all ingredients the basic procedures are to be followed, except boil to final temperature as indicated)

 (a) *Control* 114°C (237°F). Prepare the basic product formulation following the basic procedures, except boil the mixture to a final temperature of 114°C (237°F).

 (b) *Water substitution* (100%)/114°C (237°F). Prepare the basic product formulation but substitute 160 ml water in place of the 160 ml evaporated milk. Boil the mixture to a final temperature of 114°C (237°F).

 (c) *Water/milk substitution* (50%)/114°C (237°F). Prepare the basic product formulation but substitute 80 ml water plus 80 ml evaporated milk instead of the 160 ml evaporated milk. Boil the mixture to a final temperature of 114°C (237°F).

 (d) *Tartaric acid (cream of tartar)* 114°C (237°F). Prepare the basic product formulation but add 0.5 g tartaric acid before the mixture is heat treated. Boil the mixture to a final temperature of 114°C (237°F).

 (e) *Cocoa/butter* 114°C (237°F). Prepare the basic product formulation but substitute 22.5 g cocoa plus 7 g butter instead of the 28 g unsweetened chocolate. This additional butter is added in the same step as the cocoa ingredient. Boil the mixture to a final temperature of 114°C (237°F).

 (f) *Fructose* 119°C (246°F) 5 min. Prepare the basic product formulation but substitute 200 g granulated fructose instead of the 200 g granulated sucrose. When the boiling temperature reaches 112°C (234°F) continue to heat for an additional 5 min while continuously stirring.

 (g) *Fructose* 119°C (246°F) 10 min. Prepare the basic product formulation but substitute 200 g granulated fructose instead of the 200 g granulated sucrose. When the boiling temperature reaches 112°C (234°F) continue to heat for an additional 10 min while continuously stirring.

3. Beating initiation temperature (follow the basic procedures except as directed)

 (a) *Control* 113°C (236°F). Prepare the basic product formulation but do not let the mixture cool. Initiate beating at 113°C (236°F) and continue to beat until the product is firm.

 (b) *Control* 113°C (236°F). Prepare the basic product formulation but do not let the mixture cool. Initiate beating at 113°C (236°F) and continue to beat for 2 min. Stop beating and place product on waxed paper. Allow the product to finish cooling undisturbed.

(c) **Control** 80°C (176°F). Prepare the basic product formulation, let the mixture cool to 80°C (176°F) before the initiation of beating. Continue to beat until the product is firm.

(d) **Control** 60°C (140°F). Prepare the basic product formulation except let the mixture cool to 60°C (140°F) before the initiation of beating. Continue to beat until the product is firm.

ASSESSMENT

Objective Measurements

Penetrometer
Place a 1 in. cube of the product (if possible), which is on a paper plate or waxed paper, on the penetrometer platform. Using the needle attachment of the penetrometer release the needle for 30 sec. Repeat the test on the same sample and record the values and their averages on the carbohydrate crystallization data sheet. If readings were not possible, record NA (not applicable) on the data recording sheet and state why the data were not obtained.

Subjective Measurements

Descriptive
Evaluate each product for appearance, consistency, flavor, texture, and toughness. Record data on the carbohydrate crystallization data sheet.

Sensory Evaluation Ranges

Keep these ranges in mind when scoring the products. Rate the products numerically according to the attributes in Table 6.1. Keep in mind these definitions when evaluating the confections as well as the characteristics of a standard fudge product:

Flavor: The blend of taste and smell sensations evoked by a substance in the mouth.

Texture: The characteristic consistency; the overall structure; includes hardness, cohesiveness, viscosity, elasticity.

Tender: Having a soft or yielding texture, easily broken.

Tough: Having the quality of being strong or firm in texture, but flexible and not brittle; yielding to force without breaking; capable of resisting great strain without coming apart; not easily chewed or masticated.

Table 6.1. Descriptive Sensory Characteristics for Crystalline Fudge Products

CHARACTERISTICS	1		3		5
			DESCRIPTIVE RANGES		
Appearance	dull	moderately dull	slightly dull/ shiny	moderately shiny	shiny
Consistency	crumbly	moderately crumbly	slightly hard/ crumbly	moderately hard	hard
Flavor	very sweet	moderately sweet	slightly sweet bitter/ metallic	moderately bitter/ metallic	very bitter/ metallic
Texture	very coarse/ granular	moderately coarse/ granular	slightly sweet/ coarse/ creamy	moderately creamy/ smooth	very creamy/ smooth
Toughness	very tough/ rubbery	moderately tough/ rubbery	slightly tough/ tender	moderately tender	very tender

Characteristics of Standard Fudge Product

Appearance: Surface should have a high sheen; appear satiny. Color typical of confection.

Consistency: Firm enough to hold shape when cut into pieces.

Texture: Very fine, uniformly smooth, and creamy texture. Velvety feel in mouth. Very fine crystals can be identified as portion of fudge is pressed against the roof of the mouth by the tongue with other ingredients.

Flavor: Sweet, well-blended flavors with other ingredients, typical for the product.

STUDY QUESTIONS

1. What effect can be observed as the final temperature of the crystalline product is increased? Is the sugar concentration increased or decreased as the temperature rises? Why?

2. Which added ingredients influence the firmness of crystalline candies? Why do they have this effect?
3. What functions are performed by lipids in fudge?
4. Does the temperature at which beating is initiated influence the firmness of the final product? What effect does it have? Why?
5. What is a supersaturated solution? How is it produced? Why is it important in crystallization?
6. What is the purpose of adding tartaric acid to the fudge product?
7. What effect does fructose have on the fudge product? Why is the fructose product dissimiliar to the control formulation?
8. What is meant by inversion or invert sugar? Did this occur in this experiment? Why or why not?
9. At what stages of confectionary product formation do we see solutions, colloidal dispersions, and suspensions formed?

SELECTED BIBLIOGRAPHY

Birch, G. G. and Shallenberger, R. S. 1973. Configuration, conformation and the properties of food sugars. In *Molecular Structure and Function of Food Carbohydrate*, Birch, G. G. and Green, L. F. (Eds.). Applied Science Publishers, London.

Bollenback, G. N. 1969. Sugars. In *Symposium on Foods: Carbohydrates and Their Roles*, Schultz, H. W., Cain, R. F., and Wrolstad, R. W. (Eds.). AVI Publishing Co., Westport, CT.

Campbell, A. M., Penfield, M. P., and Griswold, R. M. 1979. *The Experimental Study of Food*, chapter 13. Houghten Mifflin, Boston.

Charley, H. 1982. *Food Science*, chapter 6. John Wiley & Sons, New York.

Doty, T. E. 1976. Fructose sweetness: A new dimension. *Cereal Foods World* **21**(2):62.

DuRoss, J. W. and Knightly, W. H. 1963. Key to fine candy grain extends shelf life. *Candy Ind. Confectioner J.* **121**(2):5.

Freed, M. 1970. Fructose—the extraordinary natural sweetener. *Food Prod. Dev.* **4**(1):38.

Hardy, S. I., Brennand, C. P., and Wyse, B. W. 1979. Fructose: Comparison with sucrose as a sweetner in four products. *J. Am. Dietet. Assn.* **74**:41.

Martin, L. F. 1955. Applications of research to problems of candy manufacture. *Advan. Food Res.* **6**:1.

Martin, L. F., Mack, C. H., Smith, A. G., and Fahs, F. J. 1957. *Progress in Candy. Res., Report No. 31*. National Confectioners Association, and Southern Utilization Research and Development Division, June, Agricultural Research Service, USDA, Washington, DC.

Nicol, W. N. 1971. Sweetners in food. *Process Biochem.* **6**(12):17.

Niedzielski, Z. 1983. Inhibiting effect of invert sugar on the formation of crystal nuclei in a supersaturated sucrose solution. *Gaz. Cukr.* **71**:156; *Sugar Ind. Abstr.* **26**:64 (1964).

Pariser, E. R. 1961. How physical properties of candy affect taste. *Mfg. Confect.* **41**(5):47.

Paul, P. C. and Palmer, H. H. 1972. *Food Theory and Applications*, chapter 1. John Wiley & Sons, New York.

Potter, N. N. 1978. *Food Science*, chapter 20. AVI Publishing Co., Westport, CT.
Quinlan, D. 1954. Sugar types and uses. *Food Eng.* **26**(6):85.
Saussele, H., Jr. and Fruin, J. C. 1962. 71 D.E. Corn syrup. *Mfg. Confect.* **62**(47).
Schliepake, D. 1963. Structure of aqueous sucrose solutions. *Zucker* **16**:523.
Schultz, H. W., Cain, R. F., and Wrolstad, R. W. (Eds.). 1969. *Symposium on Foods: Carbohydrates and Their Roles*. AVI Publishing Co., Westport, CT.
Van Hook, A. 1961. *Crystallization: Theory and Practice*. Reinhold, New York.
Volker, H. H. 1966. Problems in the preparation and use of dextrose fondant. *Starke* **18**:354.
Woodroof, J. G. 1960. Recent developments affecting the storage of confectionery. *Zucker Suesswarenwirt.* **13**:286.

DATA SHEET
CARBOHYDRATE CRYSTALLIZATION

NAME _____

DATE _____

VARIABLES	PENETROMETER (mm/30 sec)		
	Reading No. 1	Reading No. 2	Average
Ingredients Control			
Water (100%)			
Water/milk (50%)			
Tartaric acid			
Fructose			
Fructose/sucrose (50%)			
Cocoa/butter			
Ingredients/final T ($^\circ$C) Control/114			
Water (100%)/114			
Water/milk (50%)/114			
Tartaric acid/114			
Cocoa/butter/114			
Fructose/119—5 min			
Fructose/119—10 min			
Beating initiation T ($^\circ$C) Control/113			
Control/113—2 min			
Control/80			
Control/60			

DATA SHEET
CARBOHYDRATE CRYSTALLIZATION

NAME _____

DATE _____

VARIABLES	SENSORY CHARACTERISTICS				
	Appearance	Consistency	Flavor	Texture	Toughness
Ingredients Control					
Water (100%)					
Water/milk (50%)					
Tartaric acid					
Fructose					
Fructose/sucrose (50%)					
Cocoa/butter					
Ingredients/final T (°C) Control/114					
Water (100%)/114					
Water/milk (50%)/114					
Tartaric acid/114					
Cocoa/butter/114					
Fructose/119—5 min					
Fructose/119—10 min					
Beating initiation T (°C) Control/113					
Control/113—2 min					
Control/80					
Control/60					

Chapter 7

Experiment: Pectin Gels

THEORY

Gels are semirigid and elastic substances formed by colloidal solutions, or sols. Water, which constitutes the bulk of most gels, is immobilized in capillary spaces formed by molecules of the gelling agent. The gelling agent network traps the water in the interstices.

Under appropriate conditions a colloidal sol of pectin may become a gel. Essential ingredients of most pectin gels are pectin, sugar, acid, and water.

Pectin

There are several types of pectic substances that are derived primarily from apples and the albedo of citrus fruits. These substances are composed of galacturonic acid units combined by alpha 1,4-glycosidic linkages (see Fig. 7.1).

Pectin molecules are hydrophilic because of the great number of polar groups on the structure. In addition, the molecules contain an abundance of carboxyl groups, making them acidic and capable of salt formation. Some carboxyl groups are also esterified to methyl groups. Pectins are esterified to varying degrees, with the remainder of the carboxyl groups present uncombined or combined to form salts.

The concentration of pectin in the finished pectin gel depends upon how much water is evaporated by boiling, the proportion of sugar added to the pectin extract before evaporation begins, and the quantity of pectin added before evaporation begins. The concentration of pectin required to form a gel varies with the quality of the pectin.

Sugar

Sugar effects pectin gelation by lowering the activity of the water and dehydrating the pectin molecules. The amount of sugar used in a pectin gel depends on the quantity and quality of the pectin used. Two methods are

35

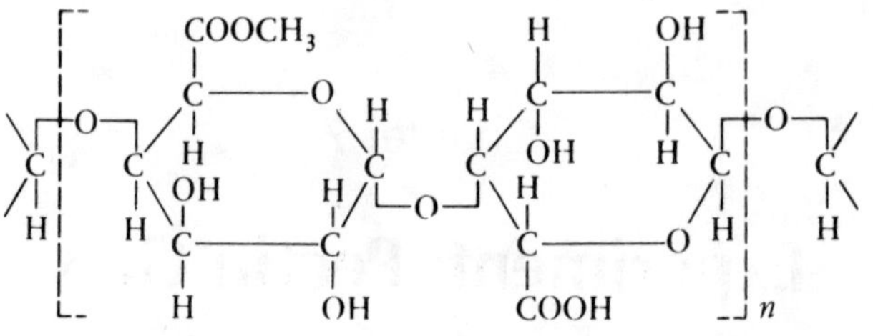

Figure 7.1. Pectin. (From Campbell, A. M., Penfield, M. P., and Griswold, R. M. 1979. *The Experimental Study of Food*, chapter 6, p. 167. Houghton Mifflin Co., Boston. Reproduced with permission.)

available to control the concentration of the sugar in the finished pectin gel. The mixture may be boiled to a predetermined weight. This is calculated on the basis of the weight of sugar combined with the fruit pectin extract. Alternately, the boiling point of the gel may be used as an index to the sugar concentration (doneness) of the pectin gel. Usually the sugar concentration required falls within the range 60–65%. This means that most pectin gels are done when the sugar concentration is sufficient to raise the boiling point of the mixture to 103–105°C (217–221°F).

Acid

Acid acts by neutralizing the charge on the carboxyl groups of pectin, thus increasing the tendency of the molecules to associate and thus to form a gel. Pectin gel formation usually is possible only below pH 3.5. As the pH is decreased below pH 3.5, the firmness of the gel increases until an optimum pH (2.8–3.4) range is reached. At pH values below the optimum, syneresis occurs. Acids such as vinegar, lemon juice, lime juice, citric acid, lactic acid, malic acid, and tartaric acid often are added in making pectin gels. The time the acid is added is another variable. Acid that is present during boiling hydrolyzes some of the sugar to invert sugar, which helps to prevent sucrose crystallization in stored pectin gels.

Water

The function of water in a pectin gel is to dissolve acid and sugar and to disperse pectin.

There are conditions where the pectin molecules are modified and thus low-sugar or no-sugar pectin gels can be produced. The more highly methylated pectins require sugar for gel formation. However, the less methylated the pectin, the lower the amount of sugar needed to produce gel formation, provided divalent cations are present. Such ions cause ionic bonding by reaction of a divalent ion with two carboxyl groups. Gel strength depends on pectin and divalent ion concentration (see Fig. 7.2).

OBJECTIVES

1. To explain the functional role of each of the following in the formation of pectin gels: high-methoxy or low-methoxy pectin, acid, sucrose or other sweetening agents, water.
2. To understand the changes in yield, appearance, and tenderness that occur in pectin gels as temperature, sweetener, acid, and pectin concentrations are varied.
3. To understand the differences between low-methoxy and high-methoxy pectin gels.
4. To demonstrate an understanding of the theory of gel formation.
5. To define the degree of methylation and the composition of the pectin molecule.
6. To explain the relationship between gel strength to the percent sag and penetrometer data.

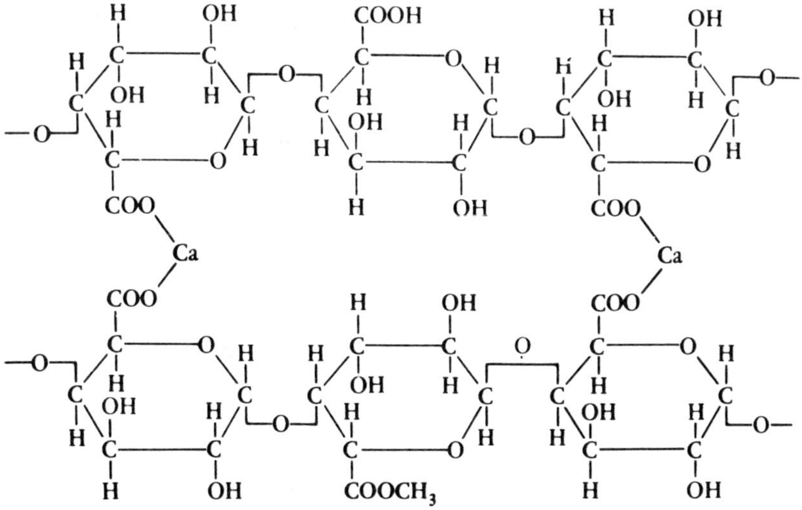

Figure 7.2. Low-ester pectin precipitated by calcium (From Campbell, A. M., Penfield, M. P., and Griswold, R. M. 1979. *The Experiemental Study of Food*, chapter 7, p. 238. Houghton Mifflin Co., Boston. Reproduced with permission.)

MATERIALS

apple juice, canned unsweetened	$4^{1}/_{2}$ gal
sucrose, white granulated	20 lb
liquid pectin (Certo)	10 boxes (2 pouches/box)
granulated pectin (Mrs. Wages)	10 boxes
aspartame (Equal)	200 packets (4 boxes)
saccharin, liquid	1–8 oz bottle
lemon juice	16 oz
saltine crackers	1 lb
saucepan, large for sterilizing jars	18
saucepans, 6–8 qt	18
jelly jars and lids	6 doz
skewers	18
beakers, 250 ml	18
beakers, 50 ml	36
paraffin	1 box
aluminum foil	1 box
double boiler	1
penetrometer with flat-head plunger	1
pH meter	2
buffer standards, pH 7.0, pH 4.0	2
thermometers	18

PROCEDURES—JAR/LID STERILIZATION

1. Select four jars with lids and check for defects.
2. Wash and drain containers.
3. Sterilize jars and lids in a large saucepan containing boiling water for 10 min. Keep hot.

PRODUCT FORMULATION (BASIC): HIGH-METHOXY PECTIN GELS

apple juice, canned unsweetened	473 ml
sucrose, granulated	700 g
liquid pectin (Certo)	90 ml (1 pouch, 3 fl oz)

PROCEDURES (BASIC): HIGH-METHOXY PECTIN GELS

1. Weigh or measure all of the ingredients using top-loading balances and/or graduated cylinders.
2. Place the juice and sweetening agent into a 6–8 qt saucepan.

3. Bring the mixture to a *full boil* over high heat, stirring constantly.
4. Stir in the liquid pectin at once.
5. Stir and bring to a *full rolling boil* (a boil that cannot be stirred down).
6. *Boil hard for 1 min*, stirring constantly.
7. Remove from heat and skim off foam with a spoon.
8. Set aside 25 ml of the sample into a 50 ml beaker. Cool to 40°C (104°F). Measure pH of mixture. Record data on pectin gel data sheet.
9. Immediately ladle the mixture into two hot jars, leaving $1/2$ in. space at the top of the jars.
10. With a damp cloth, wipe any spills from the inner rim and threads of jars.
11. Quickly seal pectin gels by spooning approximately 20 ml of hot paraffin onto the hot gel surface; make sure paraffin touches all sides and prick any air bubbles.
12. Seal the jars by covering with hot lids or aluminum foil.
13. Label the products with lab section number, date, partner names, and variable(s) studied.
14. Store pectin gels in a cool, dry place until the next laboratory session, when the pectin gels will be evaluated.

VARIABLES: HIGH-METHOXY PECTIN GELS

1. Sweetening agents (follow basic procedures for high-methoxy pectin gels)
   (a) **Sucrose *(control)***. Prepare the basic high-methoxy product formulation following the basic procedures for high-methoxy pectin gels.
   (b) **Saccharin**. Prepare the basic high-methoxy product formulation but delete the sucrose and substitute 105 ml saccharin, which is equivalent to 700 g sucrose ($3^1/2$ c).
   (c) **Aspartame *(Equal)***. Prepare the basic high-methoxy product formulation without sucrose. The basic procedures for high-methoxy pectin gels are to be followed except substitute 84 g aspartame, which is equivalent to 700 g of sucrose ($3^1/2$ c). Add this sweetner after the boiling process in step 6. Stir the aspartame into the mixture until dissolved.
2. Sucrose concentrations (follow basic procedures for high-methoxy pectin gels)
   (a) ***175 g sucrose*** (25%). Prepare the basic high-methoxy product formulation using 175 g sucrose instead of 700 g sucrose.
   (b) ***350 g sucrose*** (50%). Prepare the basic high-methoxy product formulation using 350 g sucrose instead of 700 g sucrose.
   (c) ***525 g sucrose*** (75%). Prepare the basic high-methoxy product formulation using 525 g sucrose instead of 700 g sucrose.
   (d) ***875 g sucrose*** (125%). Prepare the basic high-methoxy product formulation using 875 g sucrose instead of 700 g sucrose.

(e) *1050 g sucrose* (150%). Prepare the basic high-methoxy product formulation using 1050 g sucrose instead of 700 g sucrose.

(f) *1225 g sucrose* (175%). Prepare the basic high-methoxy product formulation using 1225 g sucrose instead of 700 g sucrose.

3. Acid concentrations (follow the basic procedures for high-methoxy pectin gels)

(a) *10 ml lemon juice*. Prepare the basic high-methoxy product formulation with the addition of 10 ml lemon juice.

(b) *25 ml lemon juice*. Prepare the basic high-methoxy product formulation with the addition of 25 ml lemon juice.

(c) *50 ml lemon juice*. Prepare the basic high-methoxy product formulation with the addition of 50 ml lemon juice.

4. Pectin concentrations (follow the basic procedures for high-methoxy pectin gels)

(a) *23 ml liquid pectin* (25%). Prepare the basic high-methoxy product formulation using 23 ml liquid pectin instead of 90 ml liquid pectin.

(b) *45 ml liquid pectin* (50%). Prepare the basic high-methoxy product formulation using 45 ml liquid pectin instead of 90 ml liquid pectin.

(c) *68 ml liquid pectin* (75%). Prepare the basic high-methoxy product formulation using 68 ml liquid pectin instead of 90 ml liquid pectin.

(d) *113 ml liquid pectin* (125%). Prepare the basic high-methoxy product formulation using 113 ml liquid pectin instead of 90 ml liquid pectin.

(e) *135 ml liquid pectin* (150%). Prepare the basic high-methoxy product formulation using 135 ml liquid pectin instead of 90 ml liquid pectin.

PRODUCT FORMULATION (BASIC): LOW-METHOXY PECTIN GELS

apple juice, canned unsweetened	473 ml
aspartame (Equal)	8.5 g
granulated pectin (Mrs. Wages)	24.5 g

PROCEDURES (BASIC): LOW-METHOXY PECTIN GELS

1. Weigh or measure all of the ingredients using top-loading balances and/or graduated cylinders.
2. Place the juice and granulated pectin into a 6–8 qt saucepan.
3. Bring the mixture to a full *rolling boil* (a boil that cannot be stirred down).
4. *Boil hard for 2 min*, stirring constantly.
5. Remove from heat and add the aspartame; mix thoroughly. Skim off any foam with a spoon.

6. Set aside 25 ml of the sample into a 50 ml beaker. Cool to 40°C (104°F). Measure pH of mixture. Record data on pectin gel data sheet.
7. Immediately ladle the mixture into two hot jars, leaving $1/2$ in. space at the top of the jars.
8. With a damp cloth, wipe any spills from the inner rim and threads of jars.
9. Quickly seal pectin gels by spooning approximately 20 ml of hot paraffin onto the hot gel surface; make sure paraffin touches all sides and prick any air bubbles.
10. Seal the jars by covering with hot lids or aluminum foil.
11. Label the products with lab section number, date, partner names, and variable(s) studied.
12. Store pectin gels in a cool, dry place until the next laboratory session, when the pectin gels will be evaluated.

VARIABLES: LOW-METHOXY PECTIN GELS

1. Sweetening agents (follow the basic procedures for low-methoxy pectin gels)
    (a) *Aspartame (control)*. Prepare the basic low-methoxy product formulation.
    (b) *Saccharin*. Prepare the basic low-methoxy product formulation but delete the aspartame sweetener and substitute 12 ml of the nonnutritive sweetener saccharin.
2. Sweetener concentrations (follow the basic procedures for low-methoxy pectin gels)
    (a) *0 g aspartame* (0%). Prepare the basic low-methoxy product formulation but delete the 8.5 g aspartame.
    (b) *2.1 g aspartame* (25%). Prepare the basic low-methoxy product formulation using 2.1 g aspartame instead of 8.5 g aspartame.
    (c) *4.3 g aspartame* (50%). Prepare the basic low-methoxy product formulation using 4.3 g aspartame instead of 8.5 g aspartame.
    (d) *6.4 g aspartame* (75%). Prepare the basic low-methoxy product formulation using 6.4 g aspartame instead of 8.5 g aspartame.
3. Acid concentrations (follow the basic procedures for low-methoxy pectin gels)
    (a) *10 ml lemon juice*. Prepare the basic low-methoxy product formulation with the addition of 10 ml lemon juice added with the apple juice.
    (b) *25 ml lemon juice*. Prepare the basic low-methoxy product formulation with the addition of 25 ml lemon juice added with the apple juice.
    (c) *50 ml lemon juice*. Prepare the basic low-methoxy product formula-

tion with the addition of 50 ml lemon juice added with the apple juice.

4. Pectin concentrations (follow the basic procedures for low-methoxy pectin gels)

(a) *6.2 g granulated pectin* (25%). Prepare the basic low-methoxy product formulation using 6.2 g granulated pectin instead of 24.5 g low-methoxy granulated pectin.

(b) *12.4 g granulated pectin* (50%). Prepare the basic low-methoxy product formulation using 12.4 g granulated pectin instead of 24.5 g low-methoxy granulated pectin.

(c) *18.6 g granulated pectin* (75%). Prepare the basic low-methoxy product formulation using 18.6 g granulated pectin instead of 24.5 g low-methoxy granulated pectin.

(d) *31 g granulated pectin* (125%). Prepare the basic low-methoxy product formulation using 31 g granulated pectin instead of 24.5 g low-methoxy granulated pectin.

(e) *37.2 g granulated pectin* (150%). Prepare the basic low-methoxy product formulation using 37.2 g granulated pectin instead of 24.5 g low-methoxy granulated pectin.

ASSESSMENT

Objective Measurements

Penetrometer
Place one of the pectin gel samples on the penetrometer platform. Using the flat-head plunger attachment of the penetrometer release the plunger for 1 min. Repeat the test on the same sample. Record the values and their averages on the pectin gel data sheet.

Percent Sag
Measure the height of the second gel sample in its container by inserting a skewer and checking the distance on the measure. Loosen and unmold the pectin gel from the container and invert onto a glass plate. Measure the height. Percent sag is calculated by this formula:

$$\% \text{ sag} = \frac{\text{height in container} - \text{height out of container}}{\text{height in container}} \times 100.$$

Record data on the appropriate data sheet.

Subjective Measurements

Descriptive
Evaluate each product for flavor and tenderness. Record data on the pectin gel data sheet.

Sensory Evaluation Ranges

Keep these ranges in mind when scoring the products. Rate the products numerically according to the attributes listed in Table 7.1

Characteristics of a Standard Product

Texture: Jellies should be firm enough to hold their shape yet malleable enough to spread. Smooth, but there is a slight resistance to pressure in the mouth. No graininess.

Clarity: The product is translucent to transparent.

Color: Pleasing.

Flavor: Full flavor.

STUDY QUESTIONS

1. What are the four essential ingredients of any high-methoxy pectin gel? What is the role performed by each ingredient? Explain the roles in relation to the commonly accepted theory of gel formation.
2. What effects are noted when the content of sucrose is increased or decreased? When pectin concentration is increased or decreased? When acid concentration is increased? When low-caloric sweeteners are lowered in low-methoxy gels?

Table 7.1. Descriptive Sensory Characteristics for Pectin Gel Products

	DESCRIPTIVE RANGES				
CHARACTERISTICS	1		3		5
FLAVOR	very sweet	mod. sweet	sl. sweet bitter/ metallic	mod. bitter/ metallic	very bitter metallic
TENDERNESS	very tough/	mod. tough	sl. tough/ tender	mod. tender	very tender

3. What occurs when low-caloric sweeteners are used in place of sucrose in high-methoxy pectin gels? Why?
4. What is the pectin compositional difference between high-sugar gels and low-sugar gels?
5. What effect does final temperature have on pectin gel strength? Why is temperature an indication of when a pectin gel is done?
6. Explain the method for determining percent sag. If a reading for percent sag is higher for one gel than it is for another gel, which pectin gel is more tender?
7. Are the sensory and/or objective characteristics different for the low-methoxy pectin gels as compared to the high-methoxy pectin gels? If so, why?
8. Explain why sucrose crystals may occur in pectin gels and how this problem can be overcome.

SELECTED BIBLIOGRAPHY

Anonymous. 1983. Low caloric sweetners. *Food Engineering* 55:138.
Bender, W. A. 1959. Pectin. In *Industrial Gums*, Whistler, R. L. and BeMiller, J. N. (Eds.). Academic Press, New York.
Black, S. A. and Smit, C. J. B. 1972. The grading of low-ester pectin for use in dessert gels. *J. Food Sci.* 37:726.
Black, S. A. and Smit, C. J. B. 1972. The effect of demethylation procedures on the quality of low-ester pectins used in dessert gels. *J. Food Sci.* 37:730.
Campbell, A. M., Penfield, M. P., and Griswold, R. M. 1979. *The Experimental Study of Food*, chapters 6, 7. Houghton Mifflin Co., Boston.
Charley, H. 1982. *Food Science*, chapter 29. John Wiley & Sons, New York.
Cloninger, M. R. and Baldwin, R. E. 1970. Aspartylphenylalanine methyl ester: A low-calorie sweetener. *Science* 170:81.
Cloninger, M. R. and Baldwin, R. E. 1974. L-Aspartyl-L-phenylalanine methyl ester (aspartame) as a sweetener. *J. Food Science* 39:347.
Gilpin, G. L., Lamb, J. C., and Staley, M. G. 1957. Effect of cooking procedures on quality of fruit jelly. *J. Home Econ.* 49:435.
Gilpin, G. L., Lamb, J. C., Staley, M. G., and Dawson, E. H. 1957. Development of jelly formulas for use with fully ripe fruit and added pectin. *Food Technol.* 11:323.
Gross, M. D., Rao, V. N., and Smit, C. J. B. 1982. Direct stress–strain dynamic characteristics of low-methoxyl pectin gels. *J. Texture Studies* 13:97.
Hinton, C. L. 1940. The quantitative basis of pectin jelly formation in relation to pH conditions. *Biochem. J.* 34:1211.
Homler, B. E. 1984. Properties and stability of aspartame. *Food Technol.* 55:50.
Inglett, G. E. 1981. Sweeteners: A review. *Food Technol.* 35:37.
Joseph, G. H. 1953. Better pectins. *Food Eng.* 25:71.
Kertesz, Z. I. 1951. *The Pectic Substances*. Interscience Publishers, New York.
Larson–Powers, N. and Pangborn, R. M. 1978. Descriptive analysis of the sensory properties of beverages and gelatins containing sucrose or synthetic sweeteners. *J. Food Science* 43:47.

Lopez, A. and Li, L. H. 1968. Low-methoxyl pectin apple gels. *Food Technol.* **22**:1023.

Meyer, L. H. 1982. *Food Chemistry*, chapter 3. AVI Publishing, Westport, CT.

Owens, H. S. and Maclay, W. D. 1946. Effect of methoxyl content of pectin on the properties of high-solids gels. *J. Colloid Sci.* **1**:313.

Paul, P. C. and Palmer, H. H. 1972. *Food Theory and Applications*, chapter 4. John Wiley & Sons, New York.

Pippen, E. L., Schultz, T. H., and Owens, H. S. 1953. Effect of degree of esterification on viscosity and gelation behavior of pectin. *J. Colloid Sci.* **8**:97.

Potter, N. N. 1978. *Food Science*, chapter 18. AVI Publishing, Westport, CT.

Rees, D. A. 1969. Structure, conformation and mechanism in the formation of polysaccharide gels and networks. *Adv. in Carbohydrate Chem. and Biochem.* **24**:324.

Smit, C. J. B. and Bryant, E. F. 1968. Ester content and jelly pH influences on the grade of pectins. *J. Food Sci.* **33**:262.

Speiser, R., Copley, M., and Nutting, G. C. 1947. Effect of molecular association and charge distribution on the gelatin of pectin. *J. Phys. Chem.* **51**:117.

DATA SHEET
PECTIN GELS—HIGH-METHOXY PECTIN

NAME ____________________

DATE ____________________

VARIABLES	pH	% SAG	PENETROMETER (mm/min) Reading No. 1	Reading No. 2	Average
Sweetening agents Sucrose (control)					
Saccharin					
Aspartame					
Sucrose concentrations (%) 175 g sucrose (25)					
350 g sucrose (50)					
525 g sucrose (75)					
875 g sucrose (125)					
1050 g sucrose (150)					
1225 g sucrose (175)					
Acid concentrations 10 ml lemon juice					
25 ml lemon juice					
50 ml lemon juice					
Pectin concentrations (%) 23 ml pectin (25)					
45 ml pectin (50)					
68 ml pectin (75)					
113 ml pectin (125)					
135 ml pectin (150)					

DATA SHEET
PECTIN GELS—HIGH-METHOXY PECTIN

NAME _____

DATE _____

VARIABLES	SENSORY CHARACTERISTICS	
	Tenderness	Flavor
Sweetening agents Sucrose (control)		
Saccharin		
Aspartame		
Sucrose concen- **trations (%)** 175 g sucrose (25)		
350 g sucrose (50)		
525 g sucrose (75)		
875 g sucrose (125)		
1050 g sucrose (150)		
1225 g sucrose (175)		
Acid concentrations 10 ml lemon juice		
25 ml lemon juice		
50 ml lemon juice		
Pectin concentrations (%) 23 ml pectin (25)		
45 ml pectin (50)		
68 ml pectin (75)		
113 ml pectin (125)		
135 ml pectin (150)		

DATA SHEET
PECTIN GELS—LOW-METHOXY PECTIN

NAME _____

DATE _____

VARIABLES	pH	% SAG	PENETROMETER (mm/min)		
			Reading No. 1	Reading No. 2	Average
Sweetening agents Aspartame (control)					
Saccharin					
Sweetener concentrations (%) 0 g aspartame (0)					
2.1 g aspartame (25)					
4.3 g aspartame (50)					
6.4 g aspartame (75)					
Acid concentrations 10 ml lemon juice					
25 ml lemon juice					
50 ml lemon juice					
Pectin concentrations (%) 6.2 g pectin (25)					
12.4 g pectin (50)					
18.6 g pectin (75)					
31 g pectin (125)					
37.2 g pectin (150)					

DATA SHEET
PECTIN GELS—LOW-METHOXY PECTIN

NAME _____

DATE _____

VARIABLES	SENSORY CHARACTERISTICS	
	Tenderness	Flavor
Sweetening agents Aspartame (control)		
Saccharin		
Sweetener concen- trations (%) 0 g aspartame (0)		
2.1 g aspartame (25)		
4.3 g aspartame (50)		
6.4 g aspartame (75)		
Acid concentrations 10 ml lemon juice		
25 ml lemon juice		
50 ml lemon juice		
Pectin concentrations (%) 6.2 g pectin (25)		
12.4 g pectin (50)		
18.6 g pectin (75)		
31 g pectin (125)		
37.2 g pectin (150)		

Chapter 8

Experiment: Amylose/Amylopectin— Gelatinization and Gelation

THEORY

Starches include not only the natural starch occurring in cereals, roots, tubers, and legumes, but also include the refined and modified starches of commerce. Starches are valued as food additives because of their texture contributions to food systems, with use as a thickening agent by far the most important food application.

Several basic phenomena of starch behavior must be understood in order to comprehend the role of starch as a thickening agent: the composition of starch with respect to its linear and branched polysaccharide components (i.e., the amylose and amylopectin) and the role of these components in starch gelatinization and gelation.

Molecular Structure

Most starches contain two glucose polymers that may be found intimately associated within a single granule. Amylose is an extended linear chain of glucose units (Fig. 8.1); this component comprises 20–30% of the common starches (corn, wheat, potato, tapioca). In contrast, amylopectin is a highly branched or tree-like glucose polymer (Fig. 8.2).

Certain recessive genetic varieties of many cereal starches contain only amylopectin. These include the so-called waxy or glutinous corn and sorghum starches. At the other end of the spectrum are the high-amylose corn starches, containing 55–85% linear fraction. These differences contribute to differences in the functional performance of various starches.

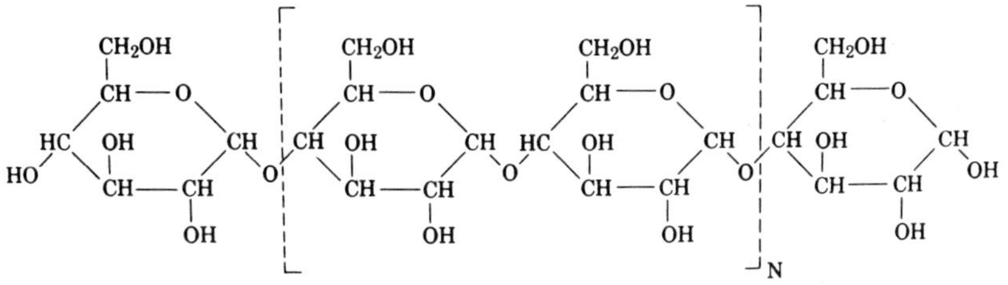

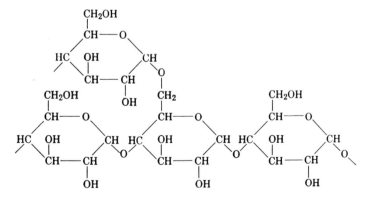

Figure 8.1. Amylose molecule. (From Paul, P. C. and Palmer, H. H. 1972. *Food Theory and Applications*, chapter 4, p. 159. Macmillan, New York. Reprinted with permission.)

Gelatinization

Gelatinization consists of the changes occurring when starch granules are heat processed in water (Fig. 8.3). At ambient temperature no obvious changes take place in native starch granules. But as heat is applied (60–70°C), the thermal energy permits some water to pass through the amorphous portion of the molecular network. As the temperature continues to increase, hydrogen bonding in the crystalline regions is disrupted. With the entire granule structure now more "loose," water uptake proceeds readily as heating continues, resulting in rapid swelling of starch granules. The temperature range over which the swelling of all the granules takes place is known as the gelatinization range, and this temperature range is characteristic of the particular variety of starch being investigated (Table 8.1). Not only

Figure 8.2. Amylopectin molecule. (From Paul, P. C. and Palmer, H. H. 1972. *Food Theory and Applications*, chapter 4, p. 160. Macmillan, New York. Reprinted with permission.)

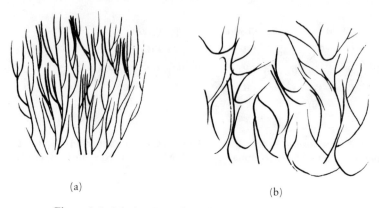

(a)   (b)

Figure 8.3. Mechanism of swelling of granular starch.

do the starch granules swell, but there is also a progressive leaching out of amylose from the swollen starch granules. Amylose that has left the granules is in colloidal dispersion. Thus, the dispersion is a sol in which the intact granules are in suspension. As the temperature rises still higher, the granules

Table 8.1. Gelatinization Ranges of Various Food Starches

SOURCE	TEMPERATURE AT LOSS OF BIREFRINGENCE (°C)		
	Initiation	Midpoint	Termination
Corn	62	66	70
Waxy corn	63	68	72
High-amylose corn (55% amylose)	67	80	—*
Grain sorghum	68	73.5	78
Waxy sorghum	67.5	70.5	74
Barley	51.5	57	59.5
Rice	68	74.5	78
Rye	57	61	70
Wheat	59.5	62.5	64
Pea (green garden peas of normal amylose content)	57	65	70
Potato	58	62	66
Potato (heat/ moisture treated)	65	71	77
Tapioca	52	59	64

SOURCE: Osman, E. M. 1967. Starch in the food industry. In *Starch: Chemistry and Technology*, vol. 2, p. 167. Whistler, R. L. and Pascall, E. F. (Eds.). Academic Press, New York. Reprinted with permission.

*Some granules are still birefringent at 100°C.

implode rather that explode. The implosion is followed by a gradual break-down into fragments.

Certain other changes occur concomitantly with the initial swelling of the starch granules. There is an increase in clarity of the starch suspension, in viscosity, and in susceptibility of the starch to hydrolysis by amylases.

Gelation

Gelation is the formation of a gel and does not occur until gelatinized starch is cooled (in other words, gelatinization must precede gelation). If the starch paste is allowed to cool, intermolecular hydrogen bonds form between amy-lose molecules (see Fig. 8.4).

The net effect is a continuous three-dimensional network of swollen gran-ules. As is the case with any type of gel, water is held enmeshed in the continuous solid network. Gel formations become progressively stronger during the first few hours after preparation. Starches containing only amylo-pectin molecules do not form gels unless the paste is very concentrated ($\geq 30\%$).

FACTORS AFFECTING AMYLOSE/AMYLOPECTIN GELATINIZATION AND GELATION

Starch as a food component is greatly influenced by numerous other ingredients in the food system, and these influences are important to the study of starch-containing foods.

Amylose/Amylopectin Concentrations
Increasing concentrations of the thickening and gelling agents results in increased viscosity and increased gel strength.

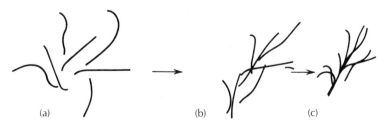

(a)   (b)   (c)

Figure 8.4. Gel formation and retrogradation: (a) Sol, (b) gel, (c) retrograded. (From Paul, P. C. and Palmer, H. H. 1972. *Food Theory and Applications*, chapter 4, p. 173. Macmillan, New York. Reprinted with permission.)

Starch Types

Depending upon amylose/amylopectin concentrations and starch purity, various starches will have different gelatinization and gelation characteristics.

Extent of Heating

Maximum viscosity depends on sufficient heating to achieve maximum starch-granule gelatinization. Maximum gel strength depends on sufficient heating to free some amylose molecules, with minimal fragmentation of granules.

Sucrose

Sucrose decreases the viscosity of the heated and cooled product in several ways. Sucrose present during the heating of starch suspensions presumably retards the hydration of starch granules by competing for water. In addition, sucrose elevates the temperature at which starch granules begin to gelatinize. Sucrose also makes the swollen granules more resistant to mechanical rupture after they are gelatinized.

Acid

Acid reduces the viscosity and gel strength of starch pastes. The acid and heat hydrolyzes starch to dextrins, which results in granule fragmentation and alteration of the exudate, thus reducing gel-forming ability. Both sugar and acid tend to make the cooked paste clearer.

OBJECTIVES

1. To understand and to explain the difference between starch gelatinization and gelation.
2. To understand the quantitative role between amylose and amylopectin in a starch granule and the subsequent viscosity and gel strength of the starch paste.
3. To explain the role of starch concentrations, starch types, high and low temperatures, sucrose, and acid upon amylose/amylopectin gelatinization and gelation.
4. To explain gelatinization and the gelation process.
5. To be able to define the terms gelatinized starch, pregelatinized starch, starch sol, waxy starch, nonwaxy starch.
6. To compare and contrast the behavior and appearance of the starches used in this experiment.

MATERIALS

ice	
sucrose, white granulated	1 cup
lemon juice	8 oz
cornstarch	$^1/_2$ lb
cornstarch, waxy	$^1/_4$ lb
rice starch	$^1/_4$ lb
tapioca, quick-cooking	$^1/_4$ lb
wheat starch	$^1/_4$ lb
potato starch	$^1/_4$ lb
white flour, all-purpose	$^1/_4$ lb
white flour, cake	$^1/_4$ lb
whole wheat flour	$^1/_4$ lb
laboratory thermometer	18
line spread chart, glass and molds	18
custard cups	36
saucepans, 1 qt	18
skewers	18
small bowls for ice water	18
graduated cylinders	18

PRODUCT FORMULATION (BASIC)

cornstarch (nonwaxy)	16 g
water	236 ml

PROCEDURES (BASIC)

1. Weigh or measure all of the ingredients using top-loading balances and/or graduated cylinders.
2. Calibrate thermometers. Adjust procedure temperatures accordingly.
3. Place starch into a 1 qt saucepan and slowly stir in water.
4. Heat the sol over medium heat while *stirring constantly* to prevent the formation of lumps and burning of the product.
5. Note the temperature at which the starch sol reaches its boiling point. Record these data on the amylose/amylopectin gelatinization and gelation data sheet.
6. Bring the starch sol to a *full boil* for 1 min, stirring constantly.
7. Remove the gelatinized starch from the heat. When the starch reaches 90°C (195°F) use 20 ml of the hot starch sol to conduct a line spread test. Record data.

8. After the line spread test has been performed, place the remaining sol in a custard cup. Cover tightly with aluminum foil and place the sol in a shallow bowl containing ice water.
9. Cool the sol until it reaches 30°C (86°F). Conduct a second line spread test on the cooled gelatinized starch using 20 ml of the mixture. Omit this test if the product gels. Record data.
10. If the starch mixture forms a gel upon cooling, determine the percent sag of the gel. Record data.

VARIABLES

1. Starch types/concentrations (for all types follow the basic procedures)
   (a) **Cornstarch (control).** Prepare the basic product formulation.
   (b) **8 g cornstarch** (50%). Prepare the basic product formulation using 8 g cornstarch instead of 16 g cornstarch.
   (c) **Cornstarch, waxy.** Prepare the basic product formulation but substitute waxy cornstarch instead of cornstarch (nonwaxy).
   (d) **8 g cornstarch, waxy** (50%). Prepare the basic product formulation but substitute 8 g waxy cornstarch instead of the 16 g cornstarch (nonwaxy).
   (e) **Rice starch.** Prepare the basic product formulation but substitute rice starch instead of cornstarch.
   (f) **8 g rice starch** (50%). Prepare the basic product formulation but substitute 8 g rice starch instead of 16 g cornstarch.
   (g) **Tapioca.** Prepare the basic product formulation but substitute tapioca instead of cornstarch. The basic procedures are to be followed.
   (h) **8 g tapioca** (50%). Prepare the basic product formulation but substitute 8 g tapioca instead of the 16 g cornstarch.
   (i) **Potato starch.** Prepare the basic product formulation but substitute potato starch instead of cornstarch.
   (j) **8 g potato starch** (50%). Prepare the basic product formulation but substitute 8 g potato starch instead of 16 g cornstarch.
   (k) **Wheat starch.** Prepare the basic product formulation but substitute wheat starch instead of cornstarch.
   (l) **8 g wheat starch** (50%). Prepare the basic product formulation but substitute 8 g wheat starch instead of the 16 g cornstarch.
   (m) **Flour, all-purpose.** Prepare the basic product formulation but substitute all-purpose flour instead of cornstarch.
   (n) **8 g flour, all-purpose** (50%). Prepare the basic product formulation but substitute 8 g all-purpose flour instead of 16 g cornstarch.
   (o) **Flour, cake.** Prepare the basic product formulation but substitute cake flour instead of cornstarch.
   (p) **8 g flour, cake** (50%). Prepare the basic product formulation but substitute 8 g cake flour instead of the 16 g cornstarch.

(q) *Flour, whole wheat.* Prepare the basic product formulation but substitute whole wheat flour instead of cornstarch.

(r) *8 g flour, whole wheat.* Prepare the basic product formulation but substitute 8 g whole wheat flour instead of 16 g cornstarch.

2. Sucrose and/or acid (for all types follow the basic procedures)

(a) *0 g sucrose (control).* Prepare the basic product formulation.

(b) *25 g sucrose.* Prepare the basic product formulation with the addition of 25 g sucrose.

(c) *50 g sucrose.* Prepare the basic product formulation with the addition of 50 g sucrose.

(d) *30 ml lemon juice.* Prepare the basic product formulation but use 30 ml lemon juice plus 206 ml water instead of 236 ml water.

(e) *60 ml lemon juice.* Prepare the basic product formulation but use 60 ml lemon juice plus 176 ml water instead of 236 ml water.

(f) *25 g sucrose/30 ml lemon juice.* Prepare the basic product formulation, adding 25 g sucrose and using 30 ml lemon juice plus 206 ml water instead of 236 ml water.

PRODUCT FORMULATION— GELATINIZATION TEMPERATURE STUDY

cornstarch (non-waxy)	32 g
water	472 ml

PROCEDURES—GELATINIZATION TEMPERATURE STUDY

1. Weigh or measure all of the ingredients using top-loading balances and/or graduated cylinders.
2. Calibrate thermometers. Adjust procedure temperatures accordingly.
3. Place starch into a 1 qt saucepan and slowly stir in water.
4. Suspend a thermometer in the pan so that the bulb is covered with the starch sol but is not touching the bottom or sides of the container.
5. Heat the sol over medium heat while *stirring constantly* to prevent the formation of lumps and burning of the product.
6. Monitor the starch sol temperature. At the temperatures specified below remove 20 ml of the hot starch sol and immediately conduct a line spread test. The temperatures used for these tests are
   (a) 70°C (158°F),
   (b) 80°C (176°F),
   (c) 90°C (194°F),
   (d) 95°C (203°F),
   (e) boiling.
7. Note the temperature at which the starch sol reaches its boiling point.

8. Record all data on the amylose/amylopectin temperature of maximum gelatinization data sheet.

VARIABLES

1. Temperature of maximum gelatinization (for all types follow the procedures for temperature study)
   (a) *Cornstarch (control)*. Prepare the product formulation for the gelatinization temperature study.
   (b) *Cornstarch, waxy*. Prepare the product formulation for the gelatinization temperature study using waxy cornstarch instead of nonwaxy cornstarch.
   (c) *Rice starch*. Prepare the product formulation for the gelatinization temperature study using rice starch instead of cornstarch.
   (d) *Tapioca*. Prepare the product formulation for the gelatinization temperature study using tapioca instead of cornstarch.
   (e) *Potato starch*. Prepare the product formulation for the gelatinization temperature study using potato starch instead of cornstarch.
   (f) *Wheat starch*. Prepare the product formulation for the gelatinization temperature study using wheat starch instead of cornstarch.
   (g) *Flour, all-purpose*. Prepare the product formulation for the gelatinization temperature study using all-purpose flour instead of cornstarch.
   (h) *Flour, cake*. Prepare the product formulation for the gelatinization temperature study using cake flour instead of cornstarch.
   (i) *Flour, whole wheat*. Prepare the product formulation for the gelatinization temperature study using whole wheat flour instead of cornstarch.

ASSESSMENT

Objective Measurements

Line Spread
Allow the gelatinized starch to spread 1 min. before taking readings. Average the four readings taken and record on the appropriate data sheet.

Percent Sag
This test is to be performed on gelled starches only. Measure the height of the gel starch sample in its container by inserting a skewer and checking the distance on the measure. Loosen and unmold the starch gel from the container and invert onto a glass plate.
Measure the height. Percent sag is calculated by this formula:

$$\% \text{ sag} = \frac{\text{height in container} - \text{height out of container}}{\text{height in container}} \times 100$$

Record data on the appropriate data sheet.

Subjective Measurements

Descriptive
Evaluate each product for appearance. Record data on the amylose/amylopectin gelatinization and gelation data sheets.

Sensory Evaluation Ranges

Keep this range in mind when evaluating the products. Rate the products numerically according to the following:

APPEARANCE	1	3	5
	opaque	sl. opaque	clear

STUDY QUESTIONS

1. What is the difference between gelatinization and gelation?
2. Describe the gelatinization and gelation process.
3. Is dextrinization a form of gelatinization? If not, explain the process of dextrinization.
4. Define the following: amylose, amylopectin, sol, solution, gelatinized starch, pregelatinized starch, syneresis, modified starch, waxy vs. non-waxy starches, retrogradation.
5. Why was the level of flour used in the experiment greater than the level of cornstarch used? Why was there a difference in the appearance of the flour-thickened paste and the cornstarch-thickened product?
6. Would the same amylose concentrations as compared to amylopectin concentrations be required to produce a product with an equivalent viscosity? Why or why not?
7. Why do high-amylopectin-content starches produce little gelation capacity and retrogradation?
8. What are the effects of separate sucrose or acid additions and the simultaneous sucrose and acid addition to starch granules in the gelatinization and gelation steps? Why?
9. Do different types of starches have different gelatinization temperature maximums? Why or why not?

SELECTED BIBLIOGRAPHY

Albrecht, J. J., Nelson, A. I., and Steinberg, M. P. 1960. Characteristics of corn-starch and starch derivatives as affected by freezing, thawing, and storage. I. Simple systems. *Food Technol.* **14**:57.

Albrecht, J. J., Nelson, A. I., and Steinberg, M. P. 1960. Characteristics of corn-starch and starch derivatives as affected by freezing, thawing, and storage. II. White sauces. *Food Technol.* **14**:64.

Banks, W., Greenwood, C. T., and Muir, D. D. 1973. The structure of starch. In *Molecular Structure and Function of Food Carbohydrate*, Birch, G. G. and Green, L. F. (Eds.). Applied Science Publishers, London.

Bean, M. and Osman, E. M. 1959. Behavior of starch during food preparation. II. Effect of different sugars on the viscosity and gel strength of starch pastes. *Food Research* **24**:665.

Campbell, A. M. and Briant, A. M. 1957. Wheat starch pastes and gels containing citric acid and sucrose. *Food Res.* **22**:358.

Campbell, A. M., Penfield, M. P., and Griswold, R. M. 1979. *The Experimental Study of Food*, chapter 9. Houghton Mifflin Co., Boston.

Charley, H. 1982. *Food Science*, chapter 8. John Wiley & Sons, New York.

Collison, R. 1968. Swelling and gelation of starch. In *Starch and Its Derivatives*, 4th ed. Radley, J. A. (Ed.). Chapman and Hall, London.

D'Appolonia, B. L. 1972. Effect of bread ingredients on starch gelatinization proper-ties as measured by the amylograph. *Cereal Chem.* **49**:532.

Foster, J. F. 1965. Physical properties of amylose and amylopectin in solution. In *Starch: Chemistry and Technology*, vol. 1: *Fundamental Aspects*, Whistler, R. L. and Paschall, E. F. (Eds.). Academic Press, New York.

Hansuld, M. K. and Briant, A. M. 1954. The effect of citric acid on selected edible starches and flours. *Food Res.* **19**:581.

Heckman, E. 1977. Starch and its modifications for the food industry. In *Food Colloids*, Graham, H. D. (Ed.). AVI Publishing, Westport, CT.

Hester, E. E., Briant, A. M., and Personius, C. J. 1956. The effect of sucrose on the properties of some starches and flours. *Cereal Chem.* **33**:91.

Kilborn, K. H., Preston, K. R., and Tipples, K. H. 1982. Implications of the term "strength" as related to wheat and flour quality. *Bakers Digest* **48**:53.

Kulp, K. 1972. Physicochemical properties of starches of wheats and flours. *Cereal Chem.* **49**:697.

Medcalf, D. G. and Gilles, K. A. 1965. Wheat starches. I. Comparison of physico-chemical properties. *Cereal Chem.* **42**:558.

Meyer, L. H. 1982. *Food Chemistry*, chapter 3. AVI Publishing, Westport, CT.

Osman, E. M. and Mootse, G. 1958. Behavior of starch during food preparation. I. Some properties of starch–water systems. *Food Res.* **23**:554.

Ott, M. and Hester, E. E. 1965. Gel formation as related to concentration of amylose and degree of starch swelling. *Cereal Chem.* **42**:476.

Paul, P. C. and Palmer, H. H. 1972. *Food Theory and Applications*, chapter 4. John Wiley & Sons, New York.

Savage, H. L. and Osman E. M. 1978. Effects of certain sugars and sugar alcohols on the swelling of cornstarch granules. *Cereal Chem.* **55**:447.

Sollars, W. and Rubenthaler, G. 1971. Performance of wheat and other starches in reconstituted flours. *Cereal Chem.* **48**:397.

Strobel, R. 1968. Functions of the starch granule in the formation of cake structure. *Cereal Chem.* **45**:329.

DATA SHEET
AMYLOSE/AMYLOPECTIN—GELATINIZATION
AND GELATION

NAME _____
DATE _____

VARIABLES	BOILING POINT (C°)	LINE SPREAD* (mm/1 min) Hot	LINE SPREAD* (mm/1 min) Cold[†]	% SAG	APPEAR-ANCE
Starch types/concentrations Cornstarch (control)					
8 g cornstarch (50%)					
Cornstarch, waxy					
8 g cornstarch, waxy (50%)					
Rice starch					
8 g rice starch (50%)					
Tapioca					
8 g tapioca (50%)					
Potato starch					
8 g potato starch (50%)					
Wheat starch					
8 g wheat starch (50%)					
Flour, all-purpose					
8 g flour, all-purpose (50%)					
Flour, cake					
8 g flour, cake (50%)					
Flour, whole wheat					
8 g flour, whole wheat (50%)					

*Average of four readings.
[†]Omit cold line spread test if the product gels. Record NA (not applicable) and conduct % sag test.

DATA SHEET
AMYLOSE/AMYLOPECTIN—GELATINIZATION
AND GELATION

NAME _____

DATE _____

VARIABLES	BOILING POINT (C°)	LINE SPREAD* (mm/1 min) Hot	LINE SPREAD* (mm/1 min) Cold†	% SAG	APPEAR-ANCE
Sucrose and/or acid 0 g sucrose (control)					
25 g sucrose					
50 g sucrose					
30 ml lemon juice					
60 ml lemon juice					
25 g sucrose/30 ml lemon juice					

*Average of four readings.
†Omit cold line spread test if the product gels. Record NA (not applicable) and conduct % sag test.

DATA SHEET
AMYLOSE/AMYLOPECTIN—TEMPERATURE
OF MAXIMUM GELATINIZATION

NAME _____

DATE _____

VARIABLES	LINE SPREAD (mm/1 min)*					BOIL-ING POINT (C°)
	70°C (158°F)	80°C (176°F)	90°C (194°F)	95°C (203°F)	Boiling	
Temperature of maximum gelatinization Cornstarch (control)						
Cornstarch, waxy						
Rice starch						
Tapioca						
Potato starch						
Wheat starch						
Flour, all-purpose						
Flour, cake						
Flour, whole wheat						

*Average of four readings.

Chapter 9

Experiment: Lipid Absorption

THEORY

The principal uses of lipids in food systems are (a) to give textural qualities, including body and smooth mouthfeel, and flavor; (b) to act as a medium for transferring heat in cooking foods by frying; (c) for shortening or tenderizing and/or leavening; and (d) as one phase of emulsions. For the first use, flavor may be a very important deciding factor in choice, along with cost. For frying and shortening, the chemical and physical characteristics of the lipid are important. This laboratory experiment will be focusing on lipid functions in terms of a heat-transfer medium and as flavoring agents to food systems. Absorption of lipids during frying should be kept to a minimum because fat-soaked foods are less palatable and contain more calories.

Lipid Absorption

The major factors governing the amount of lipid that will be absorbed by a food system during frying follow.

Time and Temperature of Heating
Generally the longer a food is heated, the greater the lipid absorption. At low temperatures more lipid is absorbed. There will be some exceptions to this. For instance, with some foods cooked at high temperatures, coagulated material or a hardened crust may prevent greater fat absorption with longer cooking. Other foods may lose lipid during cooking. Examples might be breaded pork chops and fatty chicken. Temperature of the cooking fat affects lipid absorption indirectly. At low temperatures the tendency is to cook food longer to obtain the desired browning of the food. Lipid absorption is, therefore, increased. Cooking doughnuts for 3 min at 170°, 185°, and 200°C gave no significant differences in fat absorption (Lowe et al., 1940). The color of the doughnuts was quite different, however.

64

Total Surface Area of Food
Generally the greater the surface area, the greater the lipid absorption. In the frying of doughnuts, with other things being equal, the greater the surface area, the greater the fat absorption. The total surface area of doughnuts may be increased by stretching the dough in handling and by cracks on the surface of the dough. The thicker the doughnut is rolled, the smaller is the total surface area in proportion to the weight of the doughnut. In the frying of a fritter-type batter, the absorption of fat was greatly decreased by leaving the baking powder out of the batter (Bennion and Park, 1968). The surface area of the fritters was much less without baking powder.

Composition and Nature of Food
Different types and proportions of ingredients in a product may influence the amount of lipid absorbed in frying. Increasing the fat and/or sugar in doughnuts resulted in greater lipid absorption. Increasing the egg gave a softer dough that tended to absorb more fat. On the other hand, coagulation of the increased egg protein tended to decrease lipid absorption. The final result was the sum of these two antagonistic effects and the effect of other factors (Lowe et al., 1940). The addition of egg to a fritter-type batter containing no added shortening caused significantly greater fat absorption by the batter (Bennion and Park, 1968). Fat absorption of doughnuts was found to be less if the dough temperature was near 26°C and greater if it was near 24°C. Increased handling and rerolling of the dough decreased fat absorption (Lowe et al., 1940).

Smoking Temperature of Fat Used
At lower smoke points greater lipid absorption will occur. Lowe et al. (1940) reported a significant negative correlation between lipid absorption and the smoking point of the fat. Greater absorption occurred in doughnuts cooked in fats with lower smoking points. When lipids are heated to high temperatures, some decomposition occurs and eventually a point is reached at which visible fumes are given off. This is the *smoke point*. It is defined as the lowest temperature at which the volatile gaseous products of decomposition are being evolved at sufficient rate to be visible. Definite conditions of sample size, surface area, degree of illumination, rate of heating, and the like are specified in the official procedure of the American Oil Chemists' Society for determination of smoke point. Lipids vary in the temperature at which smoking begins. Those that smoke at low temperatures are not pleasant to use for frying because of the odor and irritating effect of the fumes. The decomposition products may also give an unpleasant flavor to the food. Hence, it is preferable to use lipids with relatively high smoking temperatures for frying (Table 9.1).

In an early study, Blunt and Feeney (1915) pointed out an inverse relation-

Table 9.1. The Smoking Temperatures of Some Edible Fats

KIND OF FAT	SMOKING TEMPERATURE (°C)	FREE ACID AS OLEIC (%)
Cottonseed oil (Wesson)	233	0.07
Snowdrift	232	0.06
Crisco	231	0.13
Leaf lard	221	0.15
Butter fat	208	0.28
Leaf lard heated 5 hr	207	0.34
Bulk lard	194	0.51
A much-used lard	190	0.61
Olive oil	175	0.92
Peanut oil, I	162	1.10
Peanut oil, II	149	1.64
Coconut oil	138	1.90

SOURCE: Blunt, K. and Feeney, C. M. 1915. The smoking temperature of edible fats. *J. Home Econ.* 7:535. Reprinted with permission of the American Home Economics Association.

ship between free fatty acid content and smoke point, lower smoke points being associated with higher acidity. Others have reported similar relationships, although smoke points are influenced by additional factors as well. These include the presence of mono- and diglycerides, the presence of excess water in fat, the continued use of lipid, the presence of liberated food particles, and use of large heating containers.

One of the changes occurring when fats are heated at high temperatures is a hydrolysis of some triglyceride molecules to produce free fatty acids and glycerol. The glycerol may then be decomposed, losing two molecules of water and forming acrolein. Acrolein, which is volatile at these high temperatures, is an aldehyde that has a sharp odor and is irritating to mucous membranes of the nose and throat and to the eye tissues.

Hydrolysis reactions involved at high temperatures are

$$\text{triglycerides} + H_2O + \text{high heat} \rightarrow \text{glycerol} + \text{free fatty acid};$$
$$\text{glycerol} + \text{heat} - H_2O \rightarrow \text{acrolein (blue smoke, pungent odor and taste)}.$$

Flavor Contributions

Lipids influence flavor, whether added for that purpose or to serve another function. Often a specific lipid is chosen for a specific use because of its unique flavor. Butter, bacon fat, and olive oil are examples. Fats also act as carriers or solvents for added food flavors.

Hazards in Using Lipids for Frying

There are certain hazards in using lipids for frying. Because fat does not boil, it may be hotter than it appears. A burn from hot fat may be severe because of the high temperature and the tendency of the lipid to cling to the skin. Another hazard in using fat, and especially for deep-fat frying, is the danger of fire. When cold, wet food comes in contact with hot fat, the water as it sinks is converted into steam, the bubbles of which may cause the lipid to overflow the container. The surface of the uncooked food should be as dry as possible, overloading the container should be avoided, and the wire basket or slotted spoon that holds the food should be lifted momentarily to prevent overflow. Use of a deep kettle reduces the hazard. Fat splashed on the unit may ignite, and thus set the contents of the container on fire. Should this happen, a lid should be put on the pan and the heat turned off. The kettle should be removed from a hot electric unit.

OBJECTIVES

1. To understand the major factors governing lipid absorption of a food system and how these factors can be manipulated to either increase or decrease lipid absorption.
2. To explain the smoke point concept and the factors influencing this physical property of a lipid.
3. To cite factors to be considered in the selection of lipids when used as a heat-transfer medium for a food system.
4. To cite reasons for selecting specific temperatures and/or avoiding temperature extremes in deep-fat frying.
5. To understand one of the dehydration degradation reactions occurring during deep-fat frying in order to produce acrolein.
6. To cite ways of extending the use life of lipids for deep-fat frying.
7. To be cognizant of the role of lipids as flavoring agents in food systems and as flavor compound absorbers.

MATERIALS

flour, all-purpose	15 lb
baking powder, double acting	14 oz
sodium chloride (salt)	$1/2$ cup
sucrose, white granulated	5 lb
eggs, whole fresh	$1 1/2$ doz
milk, fluid 2%	$1/2$ gal
nutmeg	2 oz
cinnamon	2 oz

oil, corn	4 qt
oil, soybean	1 qt
oil, olive	1 qt
oil, sesame	1 qt
oil, safflower	1 qt
oil, cottonseed	1 qt
lard	2 lb
shortening, Crisco	2 lb
shortening, Crisco (butter-flavored)	2 lb
laboratory thermometers, deep-fat frying	18
containers, used oil	4
doughnut cutters	18
skewers, wooden	18
rolling pins	18
sauce pans (1 qt)	18
rolling guides, wooden $1/2''$ thick	36
waxed paper	1 roll
cookie sheets	18
boards, cutting	18
bowls, mixing medium size	18
bowls, mixing small size	18
mixers, hand	18
fire extinguisher	1
spatulas, wide	18

PRODUCT FORMULATION (BASIC)

flour, all-purpose	294 g
baking powder	10.8 g
nutmeg	0.2 g
cinnamon	0.2 g
eggs, whole fresh	45 g
vegetable oil, corn	12.5 ml
sucrose	100 g
sodium chloride	3 g
milk, fluid 2%	118 ml
vegetable oil, corn	472 ml

PROCEDURES (BASIC)

1. Weigh or measure all of the ingredients using top-loading balances and/or graduated cylinders.
2. Calibrate thermometers. Adjust procedure temperatures accordingly.

3. Ingredient mixing
   (a) Remove 40 g of the weighed flour before proceeding with the product preparation.
   (b) Into a small-sized bowl, thoroughly combine the remaining 254 g of all-purpose flour with the baking powder, nutmeg, and cinnamon, using a hand mixer (low speed) for 30 sec. Set aside.
   (c) In a medium-sized bowl, beat for 2 min on medium speed the eggs, vegetable oil (12.5 ml), sucrose, sodium chloride, and milk until the mixture is light and fluffy.
   (d) With a wooden spoon, gradually stir the flour mixture into the liquid mixture. Mix 80 strokes.
4. Formation of product — shape
   (a) Divide the dough in half.
   (b) Dust 20 g of the reserved flour on the cutting board surface and rolling pin. Place the wooden rolling guides, vertically and parallel to each other, 7 in. apart on this surface.
   (c) Place one portion of the divided dough between the rolling guides. Use your hands to shape the dough into an oblong shape.
   (d) Roll the oblong-shaped dough with a rolling pin to obtain a uniform $1/2$ in. thickness throughout the dough.
   (e) Lightly dip the doughnut cutter into flour at the edge of the cutting board. Cut out doughnut shapes as close together as possible. Obtain at least four doughnuts.
   (f) Using a wide spatula, carefully transfer the doughnuts to a cookie sheet.
   (g) Set aside the remaining scraps of dough. Repeat the above process with the second half of the dough.
   (h) Weigh four groups of uncooked doughnuts (two products per group). Record the weights of each group on the lipid-absorption data sheet. Each group will be heated at a different temperature so be sure to label the products to avoid a mix-up!
5. Thermal processing
   (a) Place 472 ml (454 g) of the assigned oil, lard, or shortening in a 1 qt saucepan.
   (b) Attach a deep-fat fryer thermometer to a 1 qt saucepan so that the bulb will be immersed in the oil but will not touch the bottom of the container.
   (c) Gradually raise the temperature of the lipid using the medium setting of the electric range to 163°C (325°F). Throughout the frying period care must be given to maintain the fat at the specified temperature.
   (d) Each doughnut should be heated individually at the designated temperature.

   Fry group 1 doughnuts at 163°C (325°F);
   Fry group 2 doughnuts at 177°C (350°F);

Fry group 3 doughnuts at 190°C (375°F); and,
Fry group 4 doughnuts at 204°C (400°F).

Carefully transfer the doughnuts into the hot fat using a wide spatula. Be careful not to splash the fat! Monitor the length of time required to cook each doughnut to obtain a product that is medium brown in color. Record these data and their average on the lipid-absorption data sheet. Use a wooden skewer to turn the product over and to remove the product when cooked.

(e) Place the cooked products in their respective groups on waxed paper.
(f) Weigh each group of cooked products. Record the group weights on the lipid-absorption data sheet.
(g) Now the scraps of remaining dough can be cooked for your own enjoyment!

VARIABLES

1. Processing lipids (for all lipids follow the basic procedures, except use lipid cooking medium specified)

(a) *Oil, corn (control).* Prepare the basic product formulation.
(b) *Oil, soybean.* Prepare the basic product formulation. Use 472 ml soybean oil instead of 472 ml corn oil as the lipid cooking medium.
(c) *Oil, safflower.* Prepare the basic product formulation. Use 472 ml safflower oil instead of 472 ml corn oil as the lipid cooking medium.
(d) *Oil, cottonseed.* Prepare the basic product formulation. Use 472 ml cottonseed oil instead of 472 ml corn oil as the lipid cooking medium.
(e) *Oil, olive.* Prepare the basic product formulation. Use 472 ml olive oil instead of 472 ml corn oil as the lipid cooking medium.
(f) *Oil, sesame.* Prepare the basic product formulation. Use 472 ml sesame oil instead of 472 ml corn oil as the lipid cooking medium.
(g) *Lard.* Prepare the basic product formulation. Use 454 g lard instead of 472 ml corn oil as the lipid cooking medium.
(h) *Shortening, Crisco.* Prepare the basic product formulation. Use 454 g shortening instead of 472 ml corn oil as the lipid cooking medium.
(i) *Shortening, Crisco (butter flavored).* Prepare the basic product formulation. Use 454 g butter-flavored shortening instead of 472 ml corn oil as the lipid cooking medium.

ASSESSMENT

Objective Measurements

Percent Lipid Absorption
Measure the weight of each group of doughnuts before and after frying. The formula to calculate the percentage lipid absorption of each group of products at each of the heating temperatures used in this study is:

$$\% \text{ lipid absorption} =$$

$$\frac{\text{cooked group weight (g)} - \text{uncooked group weight (g)}}{\text{uncooked group weight (g)}} \times 100.$$

Record the values on the lipid-absorption data sheet.

Subjective Measurements

Acceptance/Preference
Evaluate one of the products heated in each of the oils in terms of how much you *like* or *dislike* the sample you have tasted. Use the following hedonic scale. Keep in mind that you are the judge. You are the only one who can tell what you like. Nobody knows whether this product should be considered good, bad, or indifferent. An honest expression of your personal feeling will help us to decide.

_____ like extremely (7)
_____ like moderately (6)
_____ like slightly (5)
_____ neither like / dislike (4)
_____ dislike slightly (3)
_____ dislike moderately (2)
_____ dislike extremely (1)

Record your response on the lipid-absorption data sheet.

STUDY QUESTIONS

1. Were all of the lipids used appropriate for deep-fat frying? Why or why not?
2. Was there a difference in the percentage lipid absorption with the different (a) lipids, (b) temperatures? If so, why?
3. Were there any flavor changes among the products heated in the various lipids? Why?
4. Explain what happens physically and chemically to the lipid in the process of heating and/or deep-fat frying.
5. Which lipid(s) are best suited for deep-fat-frying doughnuts? Which are the least suitable? Why?
6. What are the major factors governing lipid absorption of a food system? How are these factors manipulated to either increase or decrease lipid absorption?
7. What is smoke point? What factors influence this physical property of the lipid?

8. What criteria should be used in the selection of lipids when used as a heat-transfer medium for a food system? Why?
9. In what ways can the usefulness of lipids for deep-fat frying be improved or extended?
10. Discuss the mechanism to produce acrolein. How can acrolein production be reduced?

SELECTED BIBLIOGRAPHY

Bean, M. L., Sugihara, T. F., and Kline, L. 1963. Some characteristics of yolk solids affecting their performance in cake doughnuts. I. Effects of yolk type, level, and contamination with white. *Cereal Chem.* **40**:10.

Bennion, M. 1967. Effect of batter ingredients on changes in fatty acid composition of fats used for frying. *Food Technol.* **21**:1638.

Bennion, M. and Hanning, F. 1956. Effect of different fats and oils and their modification on changes during frying. *Food Technol.* **10**:229.

Bennion, M. and Park, R. L. 1968. Changes in frying fats with different foods. *J. Am. Dietet. Assoc.* **52**:308.

Blunt, K. and Feeney, C. M. 1915. The smoking temperature of edible fats. *J. Home Econ.* **7**:535.

Campbell, A. M., Penfield, M. P., and Griswold, R. M. 1979. *The Experimental Study of Food*, chapter 8. Houghton Mifflin Co., Boston.

Charley, H. 1982. *Food Science*, chapter 14. John Wiley & Sons, New York.

Crampton, E. W., Common, R. H., Pritchard, E. T., and Farmer, F. A. 1956. Studies to determine the nature of the damage to the nutritive value of some vegetable oils from heat treatment. IV. Ethyl esters of heat-polymerized linseed, soybean, and sunflower seed oils. *J. Nutr.* **60**:13.

Firestone, D., Horvitz, W., Friedman, L., and Shue, G. M. 1961. Heated fats. I. Studies of the effects of heating on the chemical nature of cottonseed oil. *J. Am. Oil Chemists' Soc.* **38**:253.

Fleischman, A. I., Florin, A., Fitzgerald, J., Caldwell, A. B., and Eastwood, G. 1963. Studies on cooking fats and oils. *J. Am. Dietet. Assoc.* **42**:394.

Friedman, L., Horvitz, W., Shue, G. M., and Firestone, D. 1961. Heated fats. II. The nutritive properties of heated cottonseed oil and of heated cottonseed oil fractions. *J. Nutr.* **73**:85.

Goodman, A. H. and Block, Z. 1952. Problems encountered in the commercial utilization of frying fats. *J. Am. Oil Chemists' Soc.* **29**:616.

Hoerr, C. W. 1967. Changing the physical properties of fats and oils for specific uses. *Baker's Digest* **41**:42.

Lowe, R., Nelson, P. M., and Buchanan, J. H. 1940. The physical and chemical characteristics of lards and other fats in relation to their culinary value. III. For frying purposes. *Iowa Agric. Expt. Sta. Res. Bull.* **279**.

Krishnamurthy, R. G., Kawada, T., and Chang, S. S. 1965. Chemical reactions involved in the deep-fat frying of foods. 1. A laboratory apparatus for frying under simulated restaurant conditions. *J. Am. Oil Chemists' Soc.* **42**:878.

McComber, D. and Miller, E. M. 1976. Differences in total lipid and fatty acid composition of doughnuts as influenced by lecithin, leavening agent, and use of frying fat. *Cereal Chem.* **53**:101.

Meyer, L. H. 1982. *Food Chemistry*, chapter 2. AVI Publishing, Westport, CT.

Morgan, D. A. 1942. Smoke, fire, and flash points of cottonseed, peanut, and other vegetable oils. *Oil and Soap* **19**:193.

Perkins, E. G. 1960. Nutritional and chemical changes occurring in heated fats: A review. *Food Technol.* **14**:508.

Perkins, E. G. and van Akkeren, L. A. 1965. Heated fats. 4. Chemical changes in fats subjected to deep fat frying processes: Cottonseed oil. *J. Am. Oil Chemists' Soc.* **42**:782.

Poling, C. E., Warner, W. D., Mone, P. E., and Rice, E. E. 1960. The nutritional value of fats after use in commercial deep fat frying. *J. Nutr.* **72**:109.

Potter, N. N. 1978. *Food Science*, chapter 16. AVI Publishing, Westport, CT.

Rock, S. P. and Roth, H. 1964. Factors affecting the rate of deterioration in the frying qualities of fats. I. Exposure to air. *J. Amer. Oil Chemists' Soc.* **41**:228.

Rock, S. P. and Roth, H. 1966. Properties of frying fat. I. The relationship of viscosity to the concentration of non-urea adducting fatting acids. *J. Am. Oil Chemists' Soc.* **43**:116.

Roth, H. and Rock, S. P. 1972. The chemistry and technology of frying fat. I. Chemistry. *Baker's Digest* **46**(4):38.

Roth, H. and Rock, S. P. 1972. The chemistry and technology of frying fat. II. Technology. *Baker's Digest* **46**(5):38.

Rust, M. E., and Harrison, D. L. 1960. The effect of method of care on the frying life of fat. *Food Technol.* **14**:605.

Stern, S. and Roth, H. 1959. Properties of frying fat related to fat absorption in doughnut frying. *Cereal Sci. Today* **4**:176.

Thompson, J. A., Paulose, M. M., Reddy, B. R., Krishnamurthy, R. G., and Chang, S. S. 1967. A limited survey of fats and oils commercially used for deep fat frying. *Food Technol.* **21**:405.

DATA SHEET
LIPID ABSORPTION

NAME _____
DATE _____

VARIABLES	COOKING TIME (min)			GROUP WEIGHT (g)		ABSORPTION (%)	ACCEPTANCE/ PREFERENCE VALUE
	Product No. 1	Product No. 2	Average	Uncooked	Cooked		
1. Processing lipids (°C) (a) Oil, corn (control)							
Group 1 (163)							
Group 2 (177)							
Group 3 (190)							
Group 4 (204)							
(b) Oil, soybean							
Group 1 (163)							

74

Group 2 (177)					
Group 3 (190)					
Group 4 (204)					
(c) Oil, safflower					
Group 1 (163)					
Group 2 (177)					
Group 3 (190)					
Group 4 (204)					
(d) Oil, cottonseed					
Group 1 (163)					
Group 2 (177)					
Group 3 (190)					
Group 4 (204)					

DATA SHEET
LIPID ABSORPTION (continued)

NAME _____
DATE _____

VARIABLES	COOKING TIME (min) Product No. 1	COOKING TIME (min) Product No. 2	COOKING TIME (min) Average	GROUP WEIGHT (g) Uncooked	GROUP WEIGHT (g) Cooked	ABSORPTION (%)	ACCEPTANCE/ PREFERENCE VALUE
(e) Oil, olive							
Group 1 (163)							
Group 2 (177)							
Group 3 (190)							
Group 4 (204)							
(f) Oil, sesame							
Group 1 (163)							
Group 2 (177)							
Group 3 (190)							

Group 4 (204)								
(g) Lard								
Group 1 (163)								
Group 2 (177)								
Group 3 (190)								
Group 4 (204)								
(h) Shortening, Crisco								
Group 1 (163)								
Group 2 (177)								
Group 3 (190)								
Group 4 (204)								
(i) Shortening, Crisco (butter-flavored)								
Group 1 (163)								
Group 2 (177)								
Group 3 (190)								
Group 4 (204)								

Chapter 10

Experiment: Lipid Shortening Power

THEORY

One of the most important functions of lipids is to tenderize baked products that otherwise might be solid masses firmly held together by strands of gluten. This function is particularly important in pastry and breads, which have little or no sucrose. Lipids have a role in providing slippage in the gluten matrix. In addition, fat absorbed on surfaces of gluten proteins interferes with hydration and thus with the development of a cohesive gluten structure. Therefore, lipids may be added to doughs and batters for the purpose of producing a finished product that is tender and breaks apart easily. The strands or masses of gluten in the product are "shortened" or retarded in their development by the fat, which is insoluble in water. Lipids may be quite differently dispersed in various baked products. In shortened cakes they are often quite finely dispersed; in pastry and biscuits they may be dispersed in relatively large particles. In the mixing of pastry and biscuits, intimate mixing of the lipid with the other ingredients is deliberately avoided so that the lipid will cause layers of dough to form. These products are likely to be flaky as well as tender. However, flakiness and tenderness are different properties and may not be entirely compatible; as flour and fat are mixed more thoroughly, the product may become more tender but less flaky.

Shortening Power of Lipids

Various lipids may differ markedly in their shortening abilities. Attempts have been made to explain these differences. One theory suggests that the lipid covering the largest surface area has the greatest shortening power. Several factors affect the surface area covered by a fat. Among these are the nature of the lipid, its concentration, the temperature, and the manipulation and extent of mixing.

78

The Nature of the Lipid

The theory of shortening relating to the surface area covered by lipids has been developed from the work of Langmuir, Harkins, and their coworkers (Harkins and Cheng, 1921; Harkins et al., 1920; Langmuir, 1917) on cohesion, adhesion, interfacial tension, and molecular attraction between water and organic liquids. It has been suggested that the greater tenderizing power of unsaturated liquid lipids in such products as pastry may be due to a greater spreading of the liquid fat over the flour surface because of the attraction of the double bonds. The unsaturated fatty acids cover much greater areas per molecule than the saturated fatty acids. Apparently some of the double bonds are attracted to and held to the surface of the water. The plasticity of a lipid is also related to its shortening power (Hornstein et al., 1943). In a plastic or moldable fat, such as lard and hydrogenated vegetable shortenings, both solid and liquid phases are present. Depending on the fatty-acid composition and distribution, as much as 70–85% of the glycerides may be liquid and only about 15–30% crystallized in solid form at ordinary temperatures. Both chemical composition and physical structure affect the liquid/solid ratio and thus the plasticity of a lipid. The size of the crystals in the solid phase, which for a given fat will be affected by the conditions of crystallization, also affects plasticity. More plastic lipids will presumably spread more easily and cover greater flour surface, thus effecting more shortening. Plasticity is also significant in the capacity of a lipid to incorporate air during creaming or mixing.

Concentration

If other factors are equal, the shortening power is increased as the concentration of the lipid is increased. When the concentration of lipid is relatively large in a baked product, tenderizing differences between various fats will probably be little noticed. Their smaller differences are obscured at high fat concentrations.

Temperature

At higher temperatures the plasticity of lipids is increased and the lipids become softer. The fats spread more readily and the area of flour and other ingredients covered is larger with the same amount of mixing than at lower temperatures where the fat is less plastic. This change in plasticity is related to the effect of increasing temperatures on the liquid/solid ratio of the lipid. The plasticity of some lipids is much more sensitive to temperature change than other lipids. For example, butter, natural lards, and certain commercial shortenings each present different patterns of change in plasticity with increasing temperatures. The melting points of the constituent triglycerides influence these patterns. Fats of high liquid-fat content and low high-melting-point solids content probably vary little in plasticity over ordinary temperature ranges.

At higher temperatures gluten absorbs water and develops more readily. This greater development of gluten might offset the tenderizing effect of the more mobile plastic lipid covering a greater surface area of the flour.

Manipulation

Creaming, cutting, or stirring plastic fats softens them. Lipids may then spread more easily, as indicated above. The thoroughness with which lipid is mixed with flour, the amount of stirring after liquid is added, and the manner of rolling and handling dough may also influence the spreading and the shortening power of a fat. Increased mixing or handling after the addition of liquid may increase gluten development and counteract the increased shortening resulting from greater dispersion of fat.

The creaming of plastic lipids, whereby air is incorporated, has special significance when these lipids are used as shortening agents in cakes. Air cells formed in the fat during mixing are expanded during baking by carbon dioxide and steam. When the fat is more finely dispersed in the cake batter by an emulsifier such as monoglycerides, the air cells formed in the fat are smaller and more numerous, resulting in increased cake volume (Carlin, 1944). One of the many problems in relating lipid properties to shortening power is the dependence of the tenderness of pastry on many factors in addition to the fat. Hornstein et al. (1943) compared a number of fats in pastry mixed at different temperatures and by different methods, and found that the relative shortening values of the fats depended on mixing temperature and method. Correlations between shortening value and properties of lipid also depended on mixing temperature and method. Even if control of conditions is excellent and the effects of the lipids on tenderness are obvious, interpretation frequently is difficult because of the heterogeneity and variability of fats and the interrelatedness of their chemical and physical properties. For example, if an oil performs differently from a solid fat, is the effect attributable to a difference in unsaturation, in physical state, or in crystallinity? It probably is impossible to compare two fats that differ from one another in a single respect. This is not an argument against comparing fats as to shortening power but an argument for exercising caution in interpreting results, as well as for control of experimental conditions.

OBJECTIVES

1. To understand the shortening-power concept and the factors influencing the shortening power of lipids.
2. To understand the effects of temperature and physical manipulation upon the tenderness and flakiness attributes of food systems.

3. To define and understand the differences between flakiness, tenderness, and crispness attributes of a food product.
4. To demonstrate knowledge of the relationship between high and/or low shortometer values and product tenderness.
5. To demonstrate knowledge of the index of flakiness and its relationship to the flakiness of a product.
6. To explain how a variation in lipid concentration can influence the quality attributes of a shortened product.
7. To demonstrate an understanding of how the physical and chemical properties of a lipid are related to shortening power.

MATERIALS

flour, all-purpose	4 lb
shortening	1 lb
lard	$1/2$ lb
margarine, stick	1 lb
butter	1 lb
vegetable oil	1 pt
sodium chloride (salt)	$1/2$ cup
boards, cutting	18
spatulas	18
waxed paper	1 roll
cookie sheets	18
rolling guides, wood, $1/4$ in. thick	36
pastry blenders	18
rolling pins	18
bowls, mixing, med. size	18
shortometer templates	1 doz
shortometer	1
vernier calipers	6

PRODUCT FORMULATION (BASIC)

flour, all-purpose	87 g
sodium chloride	1.5 g
shortening	47 g
water	29.5 ml

PROCEDURES (BASIC)

1. Weigh or measure all of the ingredients using top-loading balances and/or graduated cylinders.

2. Preheat the oven to 218°C (425°F).
3. Ingredient mixing
   (a) Place flour and sodium chloride into a medium-sized mixing bowl. Blend ingredients with a fork.
   (b) Add all of the lipid to the dry mixture.
   (c) Using a pastry blender, cut the fat into the dry ingredients until the particles are approximately the size of uncooked rice granules.
   (d) Add water by sprinkling it over the surface of the mixture a drop or two at a time while flipping the mixture lightly upward with a fork. Try to distribute the water evenly throughout the mixture. Continue this method until all of the water has been added.
   (e) Next, make a ball of dough by mashing the mixture together using a fork. This will take approximately 10 strokes. Do this as efficiently as possible to avoid extra manipulation of the product.
4. Formation of product — shape
   (a) Turn the dough out onto a piece of waxed paper about 12 in. in length.
   (b) Quickly manipulate the dough in the waxed paper to form a more cohesive ball. Avoid holding the dough any longer than necessary to decrease warming of the product. Set aside.
   (c) Cover cutting board with waxed paper and then place the wooden rolling guides vertically and parallel to each other 4 in. apart on this covered surface.
   (d) Place the dough between the rolling guides. Use your hands to pat out the dough into an oblong shape approximately 1 in. in thickness.
   (e) Cover the dough with a sheet of waxed paper.
   (f) Lightly roll the oblong-shaped dough with a rolling pin to obtain a uniform $1/4$ in. thickness throughout the dough. Be sure the product is not on the wooden guides after shaping is completed. This is important so that dough thickness is controlled.
   (g) Gently peel off the upper layer of waxed paper and invert the pastry onto a cookie sheet.
   (h) Remove the other layer of waxed paper and cut the pastry using the shortometer templates. Cut the rectangular shapes as close together as possible.
   (i) Prick the wafers uniformly (3 places/wafer) with a fork to avoid blistering of the product during baking. In addition, prick the dough around the edges.
5. Thermal processing
   (a) Bake at 218°C (425°F) until the color is a light golden brown.
   (b) Note the total time required to bake the pastry. Record the data on the lipid-shortening-power data sheet.
   (c) Cool the product 10 min before conducting the objective and sensory measurements.

VARIABLES

1. Lipid types (for all types follow the basic procedures)
   (a) **Shortening (control)**. Prepare the basic product formulation.
   (b) **Lard**. Prepare the basic product formulation using 47 g lard instead of 47 g shortening.
   (c) **Margarine**. Prepare the basic product formulation using 47 g margarine instead of 47 g shortening.
   (d) **Butter**. Prepare the basic product formulation using 47 g butter instead of 47 g shortening.
   (e) **Oil**. Prepare the basic product formulation using 49 ml vegetable oil instead of 47 g shortening.
2. Lipid concentrations (for all types follow the basic procedures)
   (a) **Shortening** (150%). Prepare the basic product formulation using 70 g shortening instead of 47 g shortening.
   (b) **Lard** (150%). Prepare the basic product formulation using 70 g lard instead of 47 g shortening.
   (c) **Margarine** (150%). Prepare the basic product formulation using 70 g margarine instead of 47 g shortening.
   (d) **Butter** (150%). Prepare the basic product formulation using 70 g butter instead of 47 g shortening.
   (e) **Oil** (150%). Prepare the basic product formulation using 73.5 ml vegetable oil instead of 47 g shortening. The basic procedures are to be followed.
   (f) **Shortening** (75%). Prepare the basic product formulation using 35 g shortening instead of 47 g shortening.
   (g) **Lard** (75%). Prepare the basic product formulation using 35 g lard instead of 47 g shortening.
   (h) **Margarine** (75%). Prepare the basic product formulation using 35 g margarine instead of 47 g shortening.
   (i) **Butter** (75%). Prepare the basic product formulation using 35 g butter instead of 47 g shortening.
   (j) **Oil** (75%). Prepare the basic product formulation using 37 ml vegetable oil instead of 47 g shortening.
3. Lipid: water ratios (for all types follow the basic procedures)
   (a) **1.5 : 1 ratio, butter (control)**. Prepare the basic product formulation using 47 g butter instead of 47 g shortening.
   (b) **2 : 1 ratio, butter**. Prepare the basic product formulation using 44 g butter and 20.5 ml water instead of 47 g shortening and 29.5 ml water.
   (c) **3 : 1 ratio, butter**. Prepare the basic product formulation using 57 g butter and 17 ml water instead of 47 g shortening and 29.5 ml water.
   (d) **4 : 1 ratio, butter**. Prepare the basic product formulation using 62 g butter and 15 ml water instead of 47 g shortening and 29.5 ml water.

ASSESSMENT
Objective Measurements

Index to Flakiness
Stack four wafers. Measure the thickness of the stack carefully using a vernier caliper. Repeat the procedure on a second stack of four wafers and record the values and the average value on the lipid-shortening-power data sheet.

Shortometer
Raise the beam on the shortometer. Adjust the instrument to zero by moving both needles to zero. Carefully place a stack of four intact wafers across (perpendicular to) the metal platform. Measure the pressure required to break the sample. Repeat the method using a second stack of four intact wafers. Record the pressure required to break each stack and the average value on the lipid-shortening-power data sheet.

Subjective Measurements

Descriptive
Evaluate each product in terms of flakiness and tenderness. Record data on the lipid-shortening-power data sheet.

Sensory Evaluation Ranges

Rate the products numerically according to the attributes listed in Table 10.1. Keep in mind these definitions when evaluating the products as well as the characteristics of a standard pastry product.

Table 10.1. Descriptive Sensory Characteristics for Shortened Pastry Products

CHARACTER-ISTICS	DESCRIPTIVE RANGES				
	1		3		5
FLAKINESS	very thick or no layers	moderately thick layers	slightly thick/thin layers	moderately thin layers	very thin layers
TENDERNESS	very tough/ crumbly	moderately tough/ crumbly	slightly tough/ crumbly	tender	very tender

Characteristics of Standard Product

Appearance: Light, golden brown color; slightly blistered surface.
Flakiness: Thin layers of baked dough; gas cells should be medium large.
Tenderness: Pastry should "melt in the mouth"; there should be little resistance when bitten or when cut with a fork.
Flavor/General: Crisp, dry, and tender; delicate flavor influenced by the acceptability and type of fat used.

STUDY QUESTIONS

1. Compare the lipid and water content of butter, margarine, lard, and shortening. What meaning does this have for formulations of pastries when the different fats are to be used?
2. What is the interrelationship between flakiness and tenderness? Which lipid gave the most flaky pastry? Which is the least flaky? Why?
3. Is there any apparent difference in the tenderness in pastries made with different lipids? If so, which is the most tender? Which is the least tender? Explain the reason for this.
4. Is it possible to make a satisfactory pastry using butter? Using margarine? If so, what changes should be recommended from the basic formulation? Are there advantages to using butter in pastry? To using margarine? If so, what are they?
5. Outline the procedure for operating the shortometer. What precautions need to be taken to insure reliable results?
6. What are the advantages and disadvantages of each of the levels of fat tested? Which one fat and at which ratio seems to give the best all-around result?
7. Is there an advantage to chilling fat? A disadvantage?
8. Define flakiness, tenderness, and crispness.
9. What is shortening power? Cite factors that influence this lipid function.
10. How do temperature and physical manipulation affect the tenderness and flakiness attributes of a pastry dough?
11. What does a low value for index of flakiness mean?
12. What does a high value for the shortometer measurement indicate?

SELECTED BIBLIOGRAPHY

Carlin, G. T. 1944. A microscopic study of the behavior of fats in cake batters. *Cereal Chem.* **21**:189.
Charley, H. 1982. *Food Science*, chapter 15. John Wiley & Sons, New York.
Harkins, W. D. and Cheng, G. C. 1921. The orientation of molecules in surfaces: VI. Cohesion, adhesion, tensile strength, tensile energy, negative energy, interfa-

cial tension, and molecular attraction. *J. Am. Chemist's Soc.* **43**:35.

Harkins, W. D., Clark, S. L., and Roberts, L. E. 1920. The orientation of molecules in surfaces, surface energy, absorption, and surface catalysis: V. The adhesion work between organic liquids and water. *J. Am. Chemist's Soc.* **42**:700.

Hirahara, S. and Simpson, J. I. 1961. Microscopic appearance of gluten in pastry dough and its relation to the tenderness of baked pastry. *J. Home Econ.* **53**:681.

Hornstein, L. R., King, F. B., and Benedict, F. 1943. Comparative shortening value of some commerical fats. *Food Res.* **8**:1.

Langmuir, I. 1917. The constitution and fundamental properties of solids and liquids: II. Liquids. *J. Am. Chemist's Soc.* **39**:1848.

Matthews, R. H. and Dawson, E. H. 1963. Performance of fats and oils in pastry and biscuits. *Cereal Chem.* **49**:291.

Meyer, L. H. 1982. *Food Chemistry*, chapter 2. AVI Publishing, Westport, CT.

Paul, P. C. and Palmer, H. H. 1972. *Food Theory and Applications*, chapter 5. John Wiley & Sons, New York.

Potter, N. N. 1978. *Food Science*, chapter 16. AVI Publishing, Westport, CT.

Rose, I., Dressler, M. E., and Johnston, K. A. 1952. The effect of the method of fat and water incorporation on the average shortness and uniformity of tenderness of pastry. *J. Home Econ.* **44**:707.

Swartz, V. 1943. Effect of certain variables in technique on the breaking strength of lard pastry wafers. *Cereal Chem.* **20**:121.

DATA SHEET
LIPID SHORTENING POWER

NAME _____

DATE _____

VARIABLES	BAKING TIME (min)	FLAKINESS INDEX			SHORTOMETER			SENSORY CHARACTERISTICS	
		Stack No. 1	Stack No. 2	Avg.	Stack No. 1	Stack No. 2	Avg.	Tenderness	Flavor
Lipid Types Shortening (control)									
Lard									
Margarine									
Butter									
Oil									

(continued)

87

DATA SHEET
LIPID SHORTENING POWER (*continued*)

NAME _____

DATE _____

VARIABLES	BAKING TIME (min)	FLAKINESS INDEX			SHORTOMETER			SENSORY CHARACTERISTICS	
		Stack No. 1	Stack No. 2	Avg.	Stack No. 1	Stack No. 2	Avg.	Tenderness	Flavor
Lipid concentrations Shortening (150%)									
Lard (150%)									
Margarine (150%)									
Butter (150%)									

88

Oil (150%)									
Shortening (75%)									
Lard (75%)									
Margarine (75%)									
Butter (75%)									
Oil (75%)									
Lipid: water ratios 1.5 : 1 (control)									
2 : 1									
3 : 1									
4 : 1									

Chapter 11

Experiment: Emulsions

THEORY

Emulsions have several important functions in foods: some foods exist in nature as emulsions; some foods are, themselves, emulsifying agents; and some prepared foods depend for their consistency or structure on the development and maintenance of an emulsion. Emulsions are also used as vehicles to add flavors, to dilute ingredients, and to hide objectionable odors or tastes. Food emulsions occur naturally, as in milk, and are prepared in foods such as mayonnaise and cake batters. Starch contributes to emulsification of fat in some foods, such as gravies and sauces. Vegetable gums, which are used increasingly in formulated foods, function in many ways, including emulsification.

An emulsion has been defined as "a heterogeneous system, consisting of at least one immiscible liquid intimately dispersed in another in the form of droplets whose diameters, in general, exceed 0.1 μm. Such emulsions possess a minimal stability, which may be accentuated by such additives as surface-active agents, finely divided solids, etc." (Becher, 1965).

Emulsion Components

1. Dispersed or internal phase—consists of suspended droplets.
2. Continuous or external phase—the phase in which the droplets are suspended.
3. Emulsifiers, emulsifying agents, or surfactants—employed to keep droplets of one liquid suspended in another liquid if originally the two liquids were immiscible. Surfactants function by (a) decreasing the surface tension of one liquid over the other (the liquid with the lower surface tension becomes the continuous phase), and (b) preventing the coalescence of the droplets of the other liquid. An emulsifier positions itself at the oil/water interface to prevent coalescence of the dispersed phase. A number of different compounds can serve as emulsifying agents but they have this

90

characteristic in common: one part of the molecule has an affinity for and will dissolve in oil (a nonpolar component), and the other part of the molecule must be polar, having an affinity with water.

Various theories have been formulated to account for the development of an emulsion structure. The theory of micelle development accounts for many of the characteristics of emulsions. According to this theory, colloidal particles tend to become organized in a structure with their nonpolar groups in contact and their polar groups exposed to the liquid. Such an aggregation is termed a micelle. Preparation of emulsions usually requires energy in the form of work to reduce the size, increase the surface area, and separate the particles of the internal phase. Mechanical devices used include stirrers, beaters, homogenizers, and colloid mills.

To understand how an emulsifier prevents coalescence of droplets of immiscible liquids, consider one droplet of oil that has been sheared by the blades of a beater from a spoonful of oil that has been added. Before the droplet of oil has a chance to reunite with other droplets, molecules of an emulsifier line up around the circumference of the oil droplet. The fat-soluble part of each molecule of the emulsifier is oriented toward (and is in fact dissolved in) the outer layer of lipid molecules in the droplet. Figure 11.1 shows a diagram of such a droplet. The water-soluble portion of each molecule is oriented toward and dissolved in the continuous phase of water surrounding the droplet of oil. Molecules of emulsifier pack closely enough around the droplet of oil to form a layer one molecule thick. The protective film around emulsified oil droplets consists of at least three layers—the outermost layer of lipid molecules, the layer of emulsifier, and the innermost layer of water molecules. This protective layer of emulsifier prevents droplets of oil already emulsified from uniting with oil as it is added. Should two oil droplets already emulsified collide, the protective film prevents their coalescence. In a number of instances dispersed droplets in an emulsion are sur-

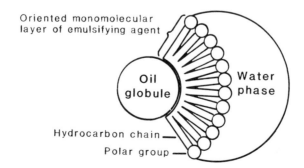

Figure 11.1. Diagram showing the orientation of emulsifying agent in oil-in-water emulsion.

rounded by a layer of electric charges, which further serves to stabilize the emulsion.

Except in margarine and butter, oil is the dispersed, or discontinuous, phase in food emulsions, and water is the dispersion medium, or continuous phase. Oil would not remain dispersed in an aqueous medium in the absence of a third phase, the *emulsifying agent*. The phospholipids of egg yolk are particularly effective emulsifying agents and function in that capacity in many foods. In mayonnaise, in which the oil concentration is particularly high, dilution of egg yolk with egg white, or total substitution of egg white for yolk, results in a product that is less viscous and less stable than the product with egg yolk.

Stability of Emulsions

Emulsion stability is affected by the same factors that influence its preparation; stability depends largely on emulsion composition and the method of preparation. Internal factors affecting stability of emulsions include the type and concentration of emulsifier, the kind and concentration of components of the dispersed and continuous phases, the viscosity of the continuous phase, the ratio of the dispersed to the continuous phases, and the particle size. The charge on the emulsion droplets promotes stability by repulsion of particles of similar charge. External factors affecting stability include agitation or shaking, evaporation (which causes coalescence of oil on the surface of oil/water emulsions), and temperature. A broken emulsion may be reformed by adding it slowly to liquid (15 ml of water for mayonnaise made with 235 ml of oil), beating the mixture after each addition, or the broken emulsion may be gradually stirred into a stable emulsion.

MAYONNAISE

Mayonnaise is a semisolid emulsified food prepared from edible vegetable oil, acidifying ingredients, and yolk-containing ingredients. It contains not less than 65% by weight of oil. It may contain sodium chloride, sweetening ingredients, and suitable harmless food seasonings or flavorings that do not impart the color of egg yolk. The acidifying ingredients may include vinegar, lemon juice, or lime juice diluted with water to not less than a specified acidity. The egg-yolk–containing ingredients may be liquid, frozen, or dried egg yolks, or whole eggs or any of the foregoing mixed with liquid or frozen egg white. It may contain calcium disodium EDTA or disodium EDTA or both, in concentrations not more than 75 parts per million by weight of the finished food, with the label statement indicating their use . . . "to protect flavor" or "as a preservative." It may be packed in an atmosphere in which air is replaced in whole or in part by carbon dioxide or nitrogen.

In making mayonnaise, the acid plus seasoning and egg yolk are combined. The shape of the bowl, which should be narrow and deep, and the blades of the beater used to incorporate the oil are important in making a good emulsion. In addition, both mustard and egg yolk lower interfacial tension between water and oil. The livetin fraction of egg yolk proteins and the micelles appear to be the most effective surface-active agents. As each portion of the oil is added, the mixture is beaten sufficiently to break up the fat into small droplets. It is important that small portions of oil be added at first and that each portion of oil be thoroughly emulsified before the next is added. Beating can be either continuous or intermittent. After some of the oil has been emulsified, the next portions are more readily emulsified. To avoid breaking the emulsion, no more oil should be added at one time than the quantity that is already emulsified.

OBJECTIVES

1. To demonstrate knowledge concerning the theory of emulsion formation and the role of each of the product formulation ingredients in the production of an emulsion.
2. To explain the role of emulsifying agents in emulsion formation and to cite several food-emulsifying agents.
3. To understand the factors involved in emulsion stability.
4. To explain how to reestablish a broken emulsion.
5. To understand why emulsions have an increase in viscosity as oil concentration is increased.
6. To evaluate the potential uses of various lipids in terms of their flavor and viscosity contributions to emulsions.

MATERIALS

acetic acid (vinegar), white	$1^1/_2$ pts
oil, olive	$^1/_2$ cup
oil, soybean	$^1/_2$ cup
oil, corn	2 qt
oil, cottonseed	$^1/_2$ cup
oil, safflower	$^1/_2$ cup
oil, sesame	$^1/_2$ cup
butter	$^1/_2$ lb
margarine, stick	$^1/_2$ lb
margarine, soft	$^1/_2$ lb
eggs, fresh	$1^1/_2$ doz
sodium chloride (salt)	$^1/_4$ c
sucrose, white granulated	$^1/_4$ c

mustard, dry	1 oz
paprika	1 oz
Lecigran*	5 g
saltine crackers	1 lb
red food coloring	1 small container
electric mixers, hand	18
mixing bowls, small	18
custard cups	36
line spread, glass and molds	12
microscope	1
microscope glass slides	5
aluminum foil	1 roll

PRODUCT FORMULATION (BASIC)

egg yolk	17 g
acetic acid (vinegar)	15 ml
sucrose	2 g
sodium chloride	1.5 g
mustard, dry	0.6 g
paprika	0.6 g
oil, corn	118 ml

PROCEDURES (BASIC)

1. Weigh or measure all the ingredients using top-loading balances and/or graduated cylinders.
2. In a small mixing bowl, place the egg yolk, acetic acid, and seasonings (sucrose, sodium chloride, dry mustard, and paprika).
3. Begin mixing these ingredients with an electric mixer on slow speed for 30 sec.
4. While continuing to mix, begin adding the oil *drop by drop* until 5 ml oil has been added. After each addition of oil, continue to beat slowly until no trace of oil is apparent before adding more oil to the emulsion.
5. After 5 ml oil has been incorporated, continue to add the oil in 1 ml increments until all of the oil has been added. Pour oil in slowly while continuously beating the emulsion.
6. Using two custard cups, place 20 ml of product into one container and the remaining product into the other container. Label the samples with lab section number, date, partner names, and variable studied.

*Obtained from Riceland Foods Inc., Little Rock, Arkansas

7. Store the samples in the refrigerator until the next laboratory session when the emulsions will be evaluated. The smaller sample will be used for a line spread test; the larger sample will be used for the subjective assessment.

VARIABLES

1. Oil types (for all types follow the basic procedures)
   (a) *Oil, corn (control).* Prepare the basic product formulation.
   (b) *Oil, olive.* Prepare the basic product formulation using 118 ml olive oil instead of 118 ml corn oil.
   (c) *Oil, soybean.* Prepare the basic product formulation using 118 ml soybean oil instead of 118 ml corn oil.
   (d) *Oil, cottonseed.* Prepare the basic product formulation using 118 ml cottonseed oil instead of 118 ml corn oil.
   (e) *Oil, safflower.* Prepare the basic product formulation using 118 ml safflower oil instead of 118 ml corn oil.
   (f) *Oil, sesame.* Prepare the basic product formulation using 118 ml sesame oil instead of 118 ml corn oil.
   (g) *Butter.* Prepare the basic product formulation using 118 ml butter instead of 118 ml corn oil. The butter should be melted and cooled to ambient temperature.
   (h) *Margarine, stick.* Prepare the basic product formulation using 118 ml margarine instead of 118 ml corn oil. The margarine should be melted and cooled to ambient temperature.
   (i) *Margarine, soft.* Prepare the basic product formulation using 118 ml soft margarine instead of 118 ml corn oil. The margarine should be melted and cooled to ambient temperature.
2. Surfactants (for all types follow the basic procedures, except as directed)
   (a) *Egg white.* Prepare the basic product formulation using 17 g egg white instead of 17 g egg yolk.
   (b) *Whole egg.* Prepare the basic product formulation using 17 g whole egg instead of 17 g egg yolk.
   (c) *0.5 g Lecigran.* Prepare the basic product formulation using 0.5 g Lecigran in place of 17 g egg yolk. Incorporate the Lecigran with the dry ingredients and *be sure* to add the oil in the increments stated in the method.
   (d) *1.0 g Lecigran.* Prepare the basic product formulation using 1.0 g Lecigran in place of 17 g egg yolk. Incorporate the Lecigran with the dry ingredients and *be sure* to add the oil in the increments stated in the method.
   (e) *1.5 g Lecigran.* Prepare the basic product formulation using 1.5 g Lecigran in place of 17 g egg yolk. Incorporate the Lecigran with the

dry ingredients and *be sure* to add the oil in the increments stated in the method.

(f) **2.0 g Lecigran.** Prepare the basic product formulation using 2.0 g Lecigran in place of 17 g egg yolk. Incorporate the Lecigran with the dry ingredients and *be sure* to add the oil in the increments stated in the method.

(g) **3.0 g Lecigran.** Prepare the basic product formulation using 3.0 g Lecigran in place of 17 g egg yolk. Incorporate the Lecigran with the dry ingredients and *be sure* to add the oil in the increments stated in the method.

3. Oil excess

(a) **Oil, corn.** Prepare the basic product formulation following the basic procedures except add an excess amount of corn oil until no more oil can be incorporated into the emulsion. Be sure to measure the total amount of oil that was added to the emulsion before it breaks. Record these data. After the emulsion breaks, put an egg yolk into a small bowl and gradually beat the broken emulsion into the yolk the same way that oil was added originally. Proceed with objective test and storage procedures.

4. Emulsion type determination

(a) **Oil, corn.** Prepare the basic product formulation following the basic procedures. After the product is made, stir 2 drops of red food coloring into 5 g product. Continue to stir until the color is uniform throughout the sample.

Microscopic examination. Place a drop of the emulsion containing the red dye on a slide. View the emulsion under the microscope and sketch the appearance. Because the red food coloring is water soluble, the areas tinted with the dye will be the acetic acid, and the untinted regions will be the oil. State whether the emulsion is oil/water or water/oil. Proceed with the objective test and storage procedures on the remaining product.

ASSESSMENT

Objective Measurements

Line Spread
Allow the product to spread 1 min. before taking readings. Average the four readings taken and record on the appropriate data sheet.

Subjective Measurements

Descriptive
Evaluate the products for the following attributes: viscosity and flavor. Record data on emulsion data sheet.

Sensory Evaluation Ranges

Keep these ranges in mind when scoring the products. Rate the products numerically according to the attributes in Table 11.1.

STUDY QUESTIONS

1. Define an emulsion. What is the difference between an oil-in-water and a water-in-oil emulsion? What type of emulsion is mayonnaise?
2. What is the role of each of the ingredients in the mayonnaise formulation?
3. Is there any difference in the stability of the mayonnaises when different fats and oils are used? If so, which is the most stable? Which is the least stable? Why?
4. Describe the flavor of each of the emulsion products. Which oil is most acceptable in flavor? Which is the least acceptable?
5. How can a broken oil-in-water emulsion be re-established?
6. Does refrigeration influence stability of emulsions? Why?
7. What is the role of Lecigran in the product formulation? Describe its action.
8. Describe the factors involved in emulsion stability.
9. Why does an increase in oil concentration in the formulation lead to an increase in product viscosity?
10. Cite examples of surfactants that are used in food systems.

SELECTED BIBLIOGRAPHY

Anonymous. 1964. *Dressings for Foods*. U.S. Food and Drug Administration, *Federal Register*, Sec. 25 (Feb. 12, 1964).
Becher, P. 1965. *Principles of Emulsion Technology*. Reinhold, New York.

Table 11.1. Descriptive Sensory Characteristics for Emulsified Products

	DESCRIPTIVE RANGES			
CHARACTERISTICS	1	3		5
VISCOSITY	very thick/ viscous	moderately thick/ viscous	slightly thick/ thin	moderately thin/ watery	very thin/ watery
FLAVOR	very undesirable	moderately undesirable	slightly undesirable/ desirable	moderately desirable	very desirable

Becher, P. 1965. *Emulsions: Theory and Practice*, 2nd ed. Am. Chem. Soc. Monograph No. 162. Reinhold, New York.
Brokaw, G. Y. 1960. Status of emulsifiers. *J. Am. Oil Chemists' Soc.* **37**:523.
Campbell, A. M., Penfield, M. P., and Griswold, R. M. 1979. *The Experimental Study of Food*, chapter 8. Houghton Mifflin Co., Boston.
Chang, C. M., Powrie, W. D., and Fennema, O. 1972. Electron microscopy of mayonnaise. *Canad. Inst. Food Sci. Technol. J.* **53**(3):134.
Charley, H. 1982. *Food Science*, chapter 16. John Wiley & Sons, New York.
Corran, J. W. 1934. Emulsification by mustard. *Spice Mill* **57**:175.
Hansen, H. and Fletcher, L. R. 1961. Salad dressings stable to frozen storage. *Food Technol.* **15**:256.
Kintner, T. C. and Mangel, M. 1952. Variation in hydrogen ion concentration and total acidity in vinegar. *Food Res.* **17**:456.
Lauridsen, J. B. 1976. Food emulsifiers: Surface activity, edibility, composition and application. *Amer. Oil Chemists' Soc. J.* **53**:400.
Meyer, L. H. 1982. *Food Chemistry*, chapter 2. AVI Publishing, Westport, CT.
Paul, P. C. and Palmer, H. H. 1972. *Food Theory and Applications*, chapter 2. John Wiley & Sons, New York.
Potter, N. N. 1978. *Food Science*, chapter 16. AVI Publishing, Westport, CT.
Pratt, C. D. and Hays, W. W. 1952. Food emulsifiers bring new highs in uniformity. *Food Eng.* **24**:109.
Sumner, C. G. 1960. Emulsions in theory and practice. *Chem. and Ind.* (March): 333.
Vincent, R., Powrie, W. D., and Fennema, O. 1966. Surface activity of yolk, plasma, and dispersions of yolk fractions. *J. Food Sci.* **31**:643.

DATA SHEET
EMULSIONS

NAME _____

DATE _____

VARIABLES	Line Spread (mm/1 min) Average of 4 Readings	OIL ADDED (ml)	SENSORY CHARAC-TERISTICS Viscosity	Flavor
Oil type Oil, corn (control)				
Oil, olive				
Oil, soybean				
Oil, cottonseed				
Oil, safflower				
Oil, sesame				
Butter				
Margarine				
Margarine, soft				
Surfactants Egg white				
Whole egg				
0.5 g Lecigran				
1.0 g Lecigran				
1.5 g Lecigran				
2.0 g Lecigran				
3.0 g Lecigran				
Oil excess Oil, corn				
Emulsion type Oil, corn	type _____			

Chapter 12

Experiment: Glutenin/Gliadin—Dough Formation

THEORY

The conversion of wheat proteins into doughs is a complex process involving all of the flour components and dough ingredients. Numerous chemical and physical changes occur.

Gluten-Forming Proteins

The gluten proteins are vital to the dough structure that develops upon hydration and manipulation of wheat flour. Although the gluten proteins, glutenin and gliadin, are separate components in the flour, these proteins interact to form gluten during dough formation. Glutenin has a large amount of intermolecular disulfide bonding plus intramolecular disulfide bonding. Gliadin has only the latter type of bonding. Neither component has the ability to form a satisfactory cohesive and an elastic dough structure independent of the other. Complexing due to hydration and physical manipulation of the flour results in gluten formation. This complexing involves breaking of some disulfide bonds and formation of new bonds. Thus, there is some disaggregation and some protein–protein interactions to ultimately form gluten. Although disulfide bonding claims much attention, hydrophobic interactions, hydrogen bonding, and ionic bonding also make important contributions to dough development during mixing. Oxidizing and reducing agents affect this interaction (see Fig. 12.1).

Lipids

Lipids are bound to the gluten protein during dough formation and binding occurs even in the absence of lipid added to the product formulation. The nature of this protein–lipid complex is unclear but lipids do contribute to

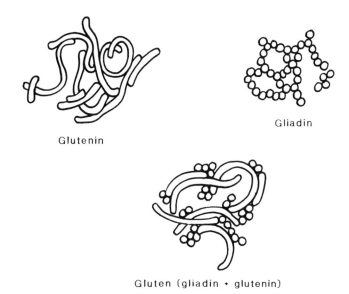

Glutenin

Gliadin

Gluten (gliadin + glutenin)

Figure 12.1. Effect of wheat protein structure on molecular association and properties.

slippage of the gluten matrix. Shortening or oils added to the dough formulation results in increased loaf volume, flavor, improved crumb grain, and reduced rate of crumb firming of the product. The total improving effect of lipids results from very small additions and within a narrow concentration range (3% of flour weight).

Carbohydrates

Starch granules become embedded in the gluten matrix during mixing. By its very presence in the gluten structure, starch has a diluting effect and possibly prevents an excessively cohesive protein structure. The starch granules partially gelatinize during heat processing and become sufficiently flexible to stretch along the gluten matrix. Thus, starch granules remove water and leave a dehydrated gluten structure that ruptures but is semirigid until coagulated by heat. The starch not only contributes to rigidity through hydration but also provides the points of weakness at which ruptures in the structure occur. Starch also adds to the structure of the final product.

Sugar components in the flour itself can be hydrolyzed by flour amylases on damaged starch. During dough fermentation these hydrolysis products provide a carbon source for yeast growth. Sugar beyond that utilized by yeast is available for carbonyl–amine browning during the baking process. If sucrose is added to the product formulation, the fermentation rate is increased.

If sucrose content exceeds 10% of the weight of the flour, fermentation is retarded by the osmotic effect of the dissolved solute on the yeast cells. Excessive sucrose may also interfere with gluten development by competing with gluten proteins for water. In addition, sucrose contributes to product browning and flavor.

Liquid

Liquid is essential for hydrolysis reactions, the hydration of the gluten-forming proteins and the gelatinization of starch granules. Water also dissolves sugar and salt, serves as a dispersion medium for yeast cells and contributes as a leavening agent in the product formulation. If fluid milk is used, it must be scalded in order to avoid a deleterious effect on dough consistency and loaf volume. The cause of this effect is not known.

Sodium Chloride

From the flavor standpoint, sodium chloride is normally used at a level of 2% of the flour's weight. Salt also has a retarding effect on yeast activity through an osmotic effect on yeast cells that controls yeast fermentation, and sodium chloride has a stiffening effect on doughs.

Yeast

The primary function of yeast is in the production of carbon dioxide for leavening and it also contributes to flavor.

OTHER FLOURS

Soy Flour

In spite of the much higher protein concentration in soy flour as compared to wheat flour, soy flour lacks dough-forming abilities. Soy proteins are primarily globulins and do not contain proteins comparable to wheat gliadin and glutenin.

The carbohydrate component of soy also differs substantially from wheat carbohydrate. Starch is lacking in soy. The carbohydrates present are fiber, dextrins, pentosans, galactans, sugars, and oligosaccharides. Because of these attributes, soy flour cannot be used as the sole flour in bread. When soy flour is combined with wheat flour in breadmaking, the soy flour makes no contribution to the viscoelastic properties of the dough. In addition, water absorption and gas retention are reduced and color and flavor are affected in proportion to the concentration of soy flour.

Rye Flour

Although the proximate composition of rye flour is rather similar to that of wheat flour and the contents of different types of proteins are not drastically different from those of wheat flour, rye-flour doughs do not behave like wheat-flour doughs. Doughs of rye flour lack a cohesive protein structure, and maturing agents do not have an improving effect. Because of the lack of strength, the doughs have poor gas-retention properties.

The carbohydrate portion of rye flour contains (in addition to starch) fiber, dextrins, sugars, hemicelluloses, and a large quantity of gummy material that apparently consists largely of pentosans. This mucilaginous gum probably is responsible for the stickiness that is characteristic of rye flour doughs and possibly interferes with development of a cohesive protein structure. "Rye breads" normally contain a rather large proportion of wheat flour because of the above properties of rye flour.

OBJECTIVES

1. To understand the interaction of wheat proteins with other flour components in terms of their roles in gluten formation.
2. To describe the role of dough ingredients in terms of their contribution to the sensory attributes (color, flavor, texture) of the final product.
3. To explain the role of physical manipulation, flour concentrations, milk, and various types of flour upon gluten formation and the sensory attributes of the final product.
4. To explain the differences between gliadin, glutenin, and gluten proteins.
5. To identify the practical use of soy, whole wheat and/or rye flours in dough-based products.

MATERIALS

flour, all-purpose	11 lb
yeast, dry granulated	18 pkgs or $^3/_4$ cups
sucrose, white granulated	$^1/_2$ cup
vegetable oil	$^1/_2$ cup
sodium chloride (salt)	$^1/_2$ cup
flour, whole wheat	1 lb
flour, soy	$^1/_4$ lb
flour, rye	1 lb
milk, fluid 2%	1 pint
laboratory thermometers	18
waxed paper	1 roll
aluminum foil	1 roll

volumeter	1
penetrometer with flat- head plunger	1
loaf pans, 3 × 6 in.	18
electric mixers, hand	18
beakers, 500 ml	18
beakers, 250 ml	18
plastic wrap	1 roll
double boilers, 2 qt.	18
bowls, medium size	18

PRODUCT FORMULATION (BASIC)

flour, all-purpose	200 g
yeast, dry	7 g
sucrose	6 g
sodium chloride	3 g
vegetable oil	4 g
water	118 ml

PROCEDURES (BASIC)

1. Preheat the oven to 220°C (425°F).
2. Weigh or measure all of the ingredients using top-loading balances and/or graduated cylinders.
3. Calibrate thermometers. Adjust procedure temperatures accordingly.
4. Heat 118 ml water to 40°C (105°F).
5. Into a 250 ml beaker add all of the yeast to 59 ml 40°C (105°F) water (taken from step 4). Allow to ferment for 10 min.
6. Place sucrose, sodium chloride, oil, and the remaining 59 ml of 40°C (105°F) water (taken from step 4) into a medium-sized mixing bowl. Stir to blend.
7. Next, add the fermented yeast dispersion into the bowl plus 50 g flour. Mix slowly for 1 min using an electric mixer until a soft paste is formed.
8. Continue to mix 125 g of the remaining flour into the soft paste. When the dough becomes too stiff for the electric mixer, remove the beaters and scrape excess dough off of them to avoid loss of product. Continue to mix by hand with a wooden spoon. Enough flour should be added to produce a dough that is irregular in shape, rough and dull in appearance, and somewhat sticky to handle. This process should take about 3 min. Because it is important to know the total amount of flour in the dough, flour to be used in kneading and shaping the dough is taken from the weighed amount that was not needed for mixing. If the original

200 g of flour are not enough to make a dough of the right consistency, weigh additional flour for use in the dough and on the bread board.

9. Turn the dough out on a lightly floured bread board and knead 100 strokes. Kneading is performed by folding the back edge of the dough to meet the front edge of the dough. Then using the heel of your hand, push the adjoining edges firmly towards the back edge. Rotate the dough 90°. Continue the fold, push, rotate pattern 100 times. The dough should become smooth and elastic. Form the elastic and smooth dough into a ball.

10. Oil a 500 ml beaker and place the dough into this container. Lightly oil the surface of the dough, then cover the beaker with waxed paper or aluminum foil.

11. Place the beaker into a water bath (top of a double boiler containing water) maintained at 35°C (95°F). Let the dough rise approximately 30 min or until doubled in bulk.

12. When the dough has doubled its volume and/or until a light finger impression remains in the dough, gently punch the dough down, turning the edges toward the center. Weigh 225 g of the dough.

13. With hands, flatten the 225 g of dough on a lightly floured board and shape into a rectangle. Form into a loaf shape by rolling from end to end. Pinch to seal the seam and the ends, and place, seam down, in an oiled pan, 3 × 6 in. Cover the loaf pan with waxed paper or aluminum foil.

14. Return the loaf pan to the water bath. The loaf pan will fit across the top of the double boiler. Cover the bread with a towel to form an environmental heated chamber maintained at 35°C (95°F). Let the bread rise in the pan until the volume has doubled. The second rising step may be shorter than the first rising step.

15. Bake the risen bread dough in the center of the oven at 220°C (425°F), for 10–15 min (until product sounds hollow when tapped with knuckles).

16. Remove the finished product from its container and cool on a wire rack for at least 10 min. before objective and sensory assessments are performed.

VARIABLES

1. Flour types (for all types follow the basic procedures)
   (a) *Flour, all-purpose (control)*. Prepare the basic product formulation.
   (b) *50 g flour, whole wheat* (25%). Prepare the basic product formulation using 50 g whole wheat flour and 150 g all-purpose flour instead of 200 g all-purpose flour.
   (c) *100 g flour, whole wheat* (50%). Prepare the basic product formula-

tion using 100 g whole wheat flour and 100 g all-purpose flour instead of 200 g all-purpose flour.

(d) **200 g flour, whole wheat** (100%). Prepare the basic product formulation using 200 g whole wheat flour instead of 200 g all-purpose flour.

(e) **50 g flour, soy** (25%). Prepare the basic product formulation using 50 g soy flour and 150 g all-purpose flour instead of 200 g all-purpose flour.

(f) **100 g flour, soy** (50%). Prepare the basic product formulation using 100 g soy flour and 100 g all-purpose flour instead of 200 g all-purpose flour.

(g) **50 g flour, rye** (25%). Prepare the basic product formulation using 50 g rye flour and 150 g all-purpose flour instead of 200 g all-purpose flour.

(h) **100 g flour, rye** (50%). Prepare the basic product formulation using 100 g rye flour and 100 g all-purpose flour instead of 200 g all-purpose flour.

(i) **50 g flours, rye, whole wheat, soy, all-purpose**. Prepare the basic product formulation using 50 g each of rye, whole wheat, soy, and all-purpose flours instead of 200 g all-purpose flour.

2. Flour concentrations (for all types follow the basic procedures)

(a) **200 g flour, all-purpose (control)**. Prepare the basic product formulation.

(b) **160 g flour, all-purpose** (80%). Prepare the basic product formulation but use only 160 g all-purpose flour instead of 200 g all-purpose flour.

(c) **240 g flour, all-purpose** (120%). Prepare the basic product formulation but use 240 g all-purpose flour instead of 200 g all-purpose flour.

(d) **280 g flour, all-purpose** (140%). Prepare the basic product formulation but use 280 g all-purpose flour instead of 200 g all-purpose flour.

3. Liquid types (for all types follow the basic procedures, except as directed)

(a) **Milk, unscalded**. Prepare the basic product formulation but substitute 118 ml unscalded milk instead of 118 ml water. In step 5, heat 59 ml of milk to be used for yeast fermentation. In step 6, 59 ml of unheated milk is to be used.

(b) **Milk, scalded**. Prepare the basic product formulation but substitute 118 ml scalded milk instead of 118 ml water. Scald (heat just below the boiling point of milk) 118 ml milk and let cool to 40°C (105°F).

4. Manipulation (for all types follow the basic procedures, except as directed)

(a) **0 Strokes, Kneading**. Prepare the basic product formulation. Do not manipulate the dough at all.

(b) **50 Strokes, Kneading** (50%). Prepare the basic product formulation. Manipulate the dough 50 strokes instead of 100 strokes.

(c) *200 Strokes, Kneading* (200%). Prepare the basic product formulation. Manipulate the dough 200 strokes instead of 100 strokes.

(d) *500 Strokes, Kneading* (500%). Prepare the basic product formulation. Manipulate the dough 500 strokes instead of 100 strokes.

ASSESSMENT

Objective Measurements

Volumeter

Wrap the loaf in plastic wrap. Place the product in the volumeter and find the volume of the product by subtracting the volume of the rapeseeds of the empty container from the volume of the rapeseeds that are surrounding the product. Repeat the measure on the same loaf and record the values and the average value on the glutenin/gliadin-dough-formation data sheet.

Penetrometer

Cut the food product in half crosswise using a serrated knife. Remove a $1/2$ in. slice from the center of the loaf and place on the penetrometer platform. Using the flat-head-plunger attachment of the penetrometer, release the plunger for 1 min. Repeat the test on a different section of the sample. Record the values and their average on the glutenin/gliadin-dough-formation data sheet.

Subjective Measurements

Acceptance/Preference

Evaluate each product in terms of how much you *like* or *dislike* the sample you have tasted based on the following hedonic scale. Keep in mind that you are the judge. You are the only one who can tell what you like. Nobody knows whether this product should be considered good, bad, or indifferent. An honest expression of your personal feeling will help us to decide.

    _____ like extremely (7)
    _____ like moderately (6)
    _____ like slightly (5)
    _____ neither like/dislike (4)
    _____ dislike slightly (3)
    _____ dislike moderately (2)
    _____ dislike extremely (1)

Record your response for each product on the glutenin/gliadin-dough-formation data sheet.

STUDY QUESTIONS

1. Is the temperature during yeast rehydration and fermentation critical? Why or why not?
2. Explain the functional role of each ingredient in the yeast-bread product formulation and its subsequent role in determining the sensory attributes of the final product.
3. Discuss in detail the glutenin/gliadin protein interactions in the formation of gluten. How do carbohydrates and lipids interact?
4. What is the effect of increasing the amount of flour in a yeast-dough formulation? Why does this result occur?
5. What is the result of using unscalded versus scalded milk as the liquid for making yeast breads? Why?
6. Discuss the role of kneading as it influences bread quality. Is it possible to knead a dough too much? Too little? What will the finished product be like if too little kneading or if too much manipulation occurs? Why do these changes happen?
7. Is it possible to substitute rye and/or soy, and/or whole wheat flours for all-purpose flour in yeast breads? If so, up to approximately what level? What might be a motivation for making such a substitution?
8. What is the result of trying to make a bread with a high percentage of rye or soy flour? What modifications can be made to make an acceptable product? Why?
9. How successful were the different flour blends that were illustrated in this experiment? Why? What avenues were suggested for further research?

SELECTED BIBLIOGRAPHY

Binger, H. P. 1965. Current studies on flour composition and baking quality. *Baker's Digest* 39(6):24.
Bloksma, A. H. 1975. Thiol and disulfide groups in dough rheology. *Cereal Chem.* 52:170.
Bloksma, A. H. 1971. Rheology and chemistry of dough. In *Wheat Chemistry and Technology*, Pomeranz, Y. (Ed.). American Association of Cereal Chemists, St. Paul, MN.
Bowman, F., Dilsaver, W., and Lorenz, K. 1973. Rational for baking wheat-, gluten-, egg-, and milk-free products. *Baker's Digest* 47(2):15.
Bushuk, W. 1974. Glutenin—functions, properties, and genetics. *Baker's Digest* 48(4):14.
Bushuk, W. and Hlynka, I. 1964. Water as a constituent in flour, dough, and bread. *Baker's Digest* 38(6):43.
Bushuk, W., Tsen, C. C. and Hlynka, I. 1968. The function of mixing in breadmaking. *Baker's Digest* 42(4):36.
Butaki, R. C. and Dronzek, B. 1980. Comparison of gluten properties of four wheat varieties. *Baker's Digest* 57(8):42.
Campbell, A. M., Penfield, M. P., and Griswold, R. M. 1979. *The Experimental Study of Food*, chapters 9, 11. Houghton Mifflin Co., Boston.

Charley, H. 1982. *Food Science*, chapters 10, 13. John Wiley & Sons, New York.

Cooley, J. A. 1965. Role of shortening in continuous dough processing. *Baker's Digest* 39(3):37.

D'Appolonia, B. L. and Gilles, K. A. 1971. Effect of various starches in baking. *Cereal Chem.* 48:625.

Eastwood, M. A. and Passmore, R. 1984. Role of starch in baked foods. *Baker's Digest* 43(5):6.

Elton, G. A. H. and Fisher, N. 1968. Effect of solid hydrocarbons as additives in breadmaking. *J. Sci. Food Agric.* 19:178.

Ewart, J. A. D. 1972. Recent research and dough visco-elasticity. *Baker's Digest* 46(4):22.

Ewart, J. A. D. 1979. Glutenin structure. *J. Sci. Food Agric.* 30:482.

Fance, W. J. 1972. *Breadmaking and Flour Confectionary*, 2nd ed. Routledge and Kegan Paul Ltd., Boston.

Greenwood, C. T. and Ewart, J. A. D. 1975. Hypothesis for the structure of glutenin in relation to rheological properties of gluten and dough. *Cereal Chem.* 52(311):146r.

Haber, T., Seyam, A. A., and Banasik, O. J. 1976. Rheological properties, amino acid composition and bread quality of hard red winter wheat, rye, and triticale. *Baker's Digest* 50(3):24.

Hoseney, R. C. 1979. Dough-forming properties. *J. Am. Oil Chemists' Soc.* 56:78A–81A.

Hoseney, R. C., Finney, K. F., and Pomeranz, Y. 1970. Functional (breadmaking) and biochemical properties of wheat flour components. VI. Gliadin–lipid–glutenin interaction in wheat gluten. *Cereal Chem.* 47:135.

Hoseney, R. C., Finney, K. F., Pomeranz, Y., and Shogren, M. D. 1971. Functional (breadmaking) and biochemical properties of wheat flour components. VIII. Starch. *Cereal Chem.* 48:191.

Hoseney, R. C., Finney, K. F., and Shogren, M. D. 1972. Functional (breadmaking) and biochemical properties of wheat flour components. X. Fractions involved in the bromate action. *Cereal Chem.* 49:372.

Hoseney, R. C., Finney, K. F., Shogren, M. D., and Pomeranz, Y. 1969. Functional (breadmaking) and biochemical properties of wheat flour components. III. Characterization of gluten protein fractions obtained by ultracentrifugation. *Cereal Chem.* 46:126.

Huebner, F. R. 1977. Wheat flour proteins and their functionality of baking. *Baker's Digest* 51(5):25.

Jackel, S. S. 1977. The importance of oxidation in breadmaking. *Baker's Digest* 51(2):39.

Jacobs, M. 1951. *The Chemistry and Technology of Food and Food Products*, Vol. II. Interscience Publishers, New York.

Jongh, G., Slim, T., and Greve, H. 1968. Bread without gluten. *Baker's Digest* 42(3):24.

Kahn, K. and Bushuk, W. 1978. Glutenin: Structure and functionality in breadmaking. *Baker's Digest* 52(2):14.

Kamman, P. W. 1961. Proofing to constant height or proofing for a definite time. *Baker's Digest* 23(4):89.

Kent, N. 1983. *Technology of Cereals*. Pergamon Press, Elmsford, NY.

Khan, M. N. and Rooney, L. W. 1977. Baking properties of oilseed flours—evaluation with a short-time dough system. *Baker's Digest* 51(3):43.

Kilborn, K. H., Preston, K. R., and Tipples, K. H. 1982. Implications of the term "strength" as related to wheat and flour quality. *Baker's Digest* 48:53.

Kilborn, R. H. and Tipples, K. H. 1972. Factors affecting mechanical dough development. I. Effect of mixing intensity and work output. *Cereal Chem.* 50:34.

Kim, S. K. and D'Appolonia, B. L. 1977. The role of wheat flour constitutents in bread staling. *Baker's Digest* 51(1):38.

Kirkpatrick, M. E., Matthews, R. H., and Collie, J. C. 1961. Use of different market forms of milk in biscuits. *J. Home Econ.* 53:201.

Knight, J. W. 1965. *Wheat Starch and Gluten*, 1st ed. Gramplin Press, London.

Kulp, K. and Lorenz, K. 1981. Starch functionality in white pan breads—new developments. *Baker's Digest* 38(6):25.

Lasztity, R. 1980. Rheological studies of a bread at the Technical University of Budapest. *J. Text. Studies* 11:81.

Magnuson, K. M. 1985. Uses and functionality of vital wheat gluten. *Cereal Foods World* 30:179.

Marston, P. E. and Wannan, T. L. 1976. Bread baking—the transformation from dough to bread. *Baker's Digest* 50(4):24.

Matthews, R. H., Sharp, E. J., and Clark, W. M. 1970. The use of some oilseed flours in bread. *Cereal Chem.* 47:181.

McDermott, E. E. 1985. The properties of commercial glutens. *Cereal Foods World* 30:169.

Mecham, D. K. 1968. Changes in flour protein during dough mixing. *Cereal Sci. Today* 13:371.

Medcalf, D. G. and Gilles, K. A. 1968. The function of starch in dough. *Cereal Sci. Today* 13:382.

Meyer, L. H. 1982. *Food Chemistry*, chapter 9. AVI Publishing, Westport, CT.

Morrison, W. R. 1976. Lipids in flour, dough, and bread. *Baker's Digest* 50:29.

Moss, R. 1974. Dough microstructure as affected by the addition of cysteine, potassium bromate, and ascorbic acid. *Cereal Sci. Today* 19:557.

Orth, R. A. and Bushuk, W. 1977. A comparative study of the proteins of wheats of diverse baking qualities. *Cereal Chem.* 23:268.

Orth, R. A., Dronzek, B. L., and Bushuk, W. 1973. Studies of gluten. IV. Microscopic structure and its relations to breadmaking quality. *Cereal Chem.* 50:688.

Paul, P. C. and Palmer, H. H. 1972. *Food Theory and Applications*, chapters 11, 12. John Wiley & Sons, New York.

Pomeranz, Y. 1966. Soy flour in breadmaking—a review of its chemical composition, nutritional value, and functional properties. *Baker's Digest* 40(3):44.

Pomeranz, Y. 1971. Composition and functionality of wheat-flour components. In *Wheat Chemistry and Technology*, Pomeranz, Y. (Ed.). American Association of Cereal Chemists, St. Paul, MN.

Pomeranz, Y. 1980. Molecular approach to breadmaking: An update and new perspectives. *Baker's Digest* 54(1):20.

Pomeranz, Y. 1968. Relation between chemical composition and breadmaking potentialities of wheat flour. In *Advances in Food Research*, Vol. 16. Academic Press, New York.

Pomeranz, Y. and Chung, O. K. 1978. Interaction of lipids with proteins and carbohydrates in breadmaking. *J. Am. Oil Chemists' Soc.* 55:285.

Pomeranz, Y., Rubenthaler, G. L., Daftary, R. D., and Finney, K. F. 1966. Effects of lipids on bread baked from flours varying widely in breadmaking potentialities. *Food Technol.* 20:1225.

Pomeranz, Y., Rubenthaler, G. L., and Finney, K. F. 1966. Studies on the mechanism of the bread-improving effect of lipids. *Food Technol.* 20:1485.

Pomeranz, Y., Shogren, M. D., and Finney, K. F. 1969. Improving breadmaking properties with glycolipids. I. Improving soy products with sucroesters. *Cereal Chem.* **46**:503.

Pyler, E. 1973. *Baking Science and Technology*, Vol. II. Siebel Publishing Co., Chicago, IL.

Rooney, L. W., Gustavson, C. B., Clark, S. P., and Cater, C. M. 1972. Comparison of the baking properties of some oilseed flours. *J. Food Sci.* **37**:14.

Schoch, T. J. 1965. Starch in bakery products. *Baker's Digest* **39**(2):48.

Shellenberger, J. A. 1981. The baking industry and wheat quality evaluation. *Baker's Digest* **56**(3):22.

Shellenberger, J. A., MacMasters, M. M., and Pomeranz, Y. 1966. Wheat carbohydrates: Their nature and function in baking. *Baker's Digest* **40**(3):32.

Sollars, W. 1958. Cookie and cake flour fractions affected by chlorine bleaching. *Cereal Chem.* **35**:100.

Sollars, W. and Rubenthaler, G. 1971. Performance of wheat and other starches in reconstituted flours. *Cereal Chem.* **48**:397.

Swanson, A. M., Sanderson, W. B., and Grindrod, J. 1964. The effects of heat treatments given to skim milk and skim milk concentrate before drying. *Cereal Sci. Today* **9**:292.

Swortfiguer, M. J. 1968. Dough absorption and moisture retention in bread. *Baker's Digest* **42**(4):42.

Tsen, C. C. 1967. Changes in flour protein during dough mixing. *Cereal Chem.* **44**:308.

Tsen, C. C. and Hoover, W. J. 1973. High-protein bread from wheat flour fortified with full-fat soy flour. *Cereal Chem.* **50**:7.

Yasunaga, T., Bushuk, W., and Irvine, G. N. 1968. Gelatinization of starch during bread-baking. *Cereal Chem.* **45**:269.

DATA SHEET
GLUTENIN/GLIADIN—DOUGH FORMATION

NAME _____

DATE _____

VARIABLES	VOLUME (cm³)			PENETROMETER (mm/min)			ACCEPTANCE/ PREFERENCE VALUE
	Reading No. 1	Reading No. 2	Average	Reading No. 1	Reading No. 2	Average	
Flour types Flour, AP (control)							
50 g flour, WW (25%)							
100 g flour, WW (50%)							
200 g flour, WW (100%)							
50 g flour, soy (25%)							
100 g flour, soy (50%)							
50 g flour, rye (25%)							

100 g flour, rye (50%)						
50 g flour, WW, Rye, soy, AP						
Flour concentrations 200 g flour, AP (control)						
160 g flour, AP (80%)						
240 g flour, AP (120%)						
280 g flour, AP (140%)						
Liquid types Milk, unscalded						
Milk, scalded						
Manipulation 0 strokes, kneading						
50 strokes, kneading						
200 strokes, kneading						
500 strokes, kneading						

113

Chapter 13

Experiment: Protein Foams

THEORY

A foam consists of bubbles of gas trapped in a liquid, with the liquid as the continuous phase and the gas bubbles as the dispersed phase. In edible foams, the gas is usually air and the liquid phase chiefly water. A foam is formed in foods usually by whipping or beating a liquid. If the surface tension of the liquid is low enough, the blades of the beater can pull the liquid around the air pockets.

Foam Formation

The foaming of egg whites is important in many food systems, contributing leavening action plus aiding in the production of products that are light in texture. Stable egg foams are essential for the production of angel cake, meringues, divinity candy, souffles, omelets, and sponge cakes. Egg white foam is a colloidal suspension consisting of air bubbles surrounded by albumen that has undergone some denaturation at the liquid–air interfaces. This denaturation, which is caused by the drying and stretching of the albumen during beating, makes some of the globulins (ovomucin and conalbumin)insoluble, thus stiffening and stabilizing the foam. The globulins are important in foam formation because these proteins contribute to viscosity and lower the surface tension. During denaturation, layers of ovomucin are sheared from the white. Ovomucin molecules coil to form hollow tubes. Then the molecules uncoil at the interface between air in the bubbles and the thinning films of liquid around them, exposing reactive R-groups. Molecules of such surface-denatured proteins unite through reactive R-groups and stabilize the foam. Excessive beating incorporates too much air, resulting in denaturation of too much ovomucin so that the protein films become thin and inelastic. Elasticity is needed, especially in baked foams, so that incorporated air can expand without breaking the cell walls before the ovalbumin is coagulated by heat. Heat coagulation gives permanence to the foam.

Factors Affecting Foaming

The time required for foam formation, the foam volume, and the foam stability are affected by many factors, which include beating method, time, temperature, egg white characteristics, pH, and the presence of other substances such as water, lipid, sodium chloride, sucrose, and egg yolk.

Type of Beater

The type of beater influences the beating rate of egg white foams and their optimum specific volume; the wires and blades of beaters differ considerably. Hand beaters prove less effective than electric mixers in foam formation. An electric mixer with a hypocycloidal action produces greater foaming than that produced by twin beaters. Blender blades cut the albumen fibers rather than incorporate air to form a foam.

Beating Time

Foam stability varies with beating time. As the time of beating the egg white is increased, foam volume first increases, then decreases. These changes are related to the increasing amounts of egg white coagulated at the air–egg interface and to the eventual breaking of egg films with excessive whipping. Like volume, the stability of egg white foam also increases and then decreases as beating time increases. Maximum stability is reached before maximum volume.

Temperature

Egg white at ambient temperature can be beaten more readily than egg white at refrigerator temperature. This may be due to a lowered surface tension at the higher temperature. It has been found that chilled egg white requires longer beating or produces less volume than that beaten at room temperature (21 °C or 70°F), whereas egg albumen warmed to 30°C (86°F) produces foams of increased volume but decreased stability.

Egg White Characteristics

When the thick and thin albumen are separated, the thin white can be beaten more readily than the thick albumen and the thin albumen produces greater foam volume. Because albumen thins as eggs are stored, albumen from stored eggs beats more quickly than white from fresh eggs. Foam volume is less for high-lysozyme egg white than for egg albumen containing less lysozyme. Reconstituted dried egg whites require a much longer time to whip than do fresh egg whites. Prior to drying, egg whites are pasteurized to eliminate salmonella microorganisms. The heating needed to make the eggs safe to eat greatly increases the whipping time. This has been attributed to damage to the lysozyme–ovomucin complex, but another reason may be the lability of conalbumin due to heat. Heat denaturation of the lysozyme–ovomucin complex, which results in a dry foam that tends to break as the blades of the beater are incorporating additional air bubbles, has also been suggested as a factor contributing to the longer beating time for dried egg whites.

pH

The pH of the egg white is important to foam formation. Tartaric acid (cream of tartar) is frequently added to lower the pH because this acid was found to be more effective in increasing foam stability than either acetic acid or citric acid. Lowering the pH changes the protein concentration at the liquid–foam interface. Tartaric acid is best added during the first portion of the beating period. The addition of acid to egg white also makes the foam more stable to heat. As foam stability is increased, shrinkage of angel food cake is decreased. The increased stability makes it possible for heat to penetrate the product and coagulate the egg white protein before the air cells collapse.

Added Ingredients

Dilution of egg white with *water*, up to 40% of the volume of the egg, increases the volume of the foam as much as would an equivalent volume of egg. However, water added to egg whites used in meringues increases leakage.

The presence of *lipid/egg yolk*, even in small amounts, interferes with the foaming of egg whites and reduces the foam volume. Data suggest that the lipoproteins lipovitellenin and lipovitellin interfere with the foaming potential of ovomucin and lysozyme. During egg storage, yolk or yolk fat does not migrate from the yolk to the albumen in amounts sufficient to affect the volumes of angel cakes prepared from such eggs.

The addition of *sodium chloride* to egg white or whole eggs before beating reduces the stability of the foam. Amounts of sodium chloride up to 1.5 g per 66 g egg white decrease volume and stability and increase whipping time for reconstituted dried egg whites. The addition of sodium chloride to fresh egg whites also lessens the stability of the foam unless heating time is increased from 6 to 9 min. With whole eggs, the addition of sodium chloride before beating results in a foam of small volume that does not form peaks. Sponge cakes made from such a foam are smaller in volume and less tender than when sodium chloride is omitted or is sifted with the flour.

Sucrose delays formation of egg white foams by delaying surface coagulation of the egg white, thus making the egg white less susceptible to overbeating. Foams to which sucrose is added are smoother and more stable than are foams without sugar, although the volume may be less. The shininess of egg white foam with added sucrose is due in part to the prevention of protein coagulation with the accompanying opaqueness.

ANGEL CAKE

The qualities desired in angel cake are good volume, tenderness, fairly even and fine texture or grain, and delicate and pleasing flavor. Optimum volume, tenderness, and texture are affected by the extent of whipping of the whites, the ingredients used, and baking conditions.

Angel cake volume depends on whipping the egg white foam to its optimum stage. The optimum foam value may be less than the maximum to which the foam can be whipped. The enclosed air and the steam produced during baking expand the foam-cell walls. Coagulation of the stretched cell walls during baking results in a tender cake of large volume. With insufficient beating, too little air is enclosed in the foam. Expansion of air and steam does not stretch the cell membranes to their full capacity, producing relatively thick cell walls in a tough cake of low volume. An overwhipped foam loses extensibility, cell walls break during baking, and a cake of low volume results.

In addition to the egg white, the essential ingredients in angel cake are acid (cream of tartar), sucrose, and flour. If tartaric acid is omitted, the cake color is yellowish, the texture coarse, the cell walls thick, and the cake tough. Flavone pigments in flour are colorless in acid or neutral media, but yellowish or yellow-green in alkaline media. Tartaric, acetic, and citric acids produce angel cakes of approximately the same texture at pH 8. At pH 6 the tartaric acid produces the least-coarse texture in cake, the acetic acid produces a coarse texture, and the citric acid produces an intermediate texture. At a lower pH in the finished cake, the relation of foam stability to texture is even more noticeable. There are two functions of acid in angel cake: (a) stabilizing the foam so that the temperature of coagulation is reached before the foam collapses, and (b) preventing the extreme shrinkage during the last part of the baking and during the cooling period.

Fine crystalline sucrose is used for angel cake because it dissolves rapidly. The optimum amount of sucrose depends somewhat on the amount of flour. Flour may vary from 0.2 to 0.4 g per gram of egg white. The smaller amount of flour gives a moist and tender cake; the larger, a drier and less tender one. Excess sucrose will prevent coagulation during baking, and the cake will fall. The crust will be sugary, crystalline, and rather dry. Part or all of the sucrose should be added before any of the flour to improve foam stability.

Cake flour is used in angel cakes as a binder and to provide gelatinized starch; it supplements the egg protein in forming the cake structure. All-purpose flour causes the cakes to shrink excessively and pull away from the sides of the pan during the last part of the baking period and during cooling because of the cohesive properties of the gluten. Such cakes are compact and have small volume. Wheat starch has been used recently in place of as much as 30% of the flour; such substitution improves cake volume and quality. Flour and starch are folded in at the end of the mixing period. Loss of volume at this stage is related to agitation of the flour–foam system. Increasing the egg or flour in angel cake increases its tensile strength; increasing the sucrose decreases the tensile strength.

Desirable cakes can be baked at a range of temperatures; the optimum baking time at a given temperature depends on the volume and shape of the pan. At high temperatures the crust sets so rapidly that cake volume is reduced; at low temperatures, the cake structure is unduly long in setting. For a given formula and altitude, the maximum internal temperature is nearly the same regardless of the oven temperature. Continued baking after the maximum temperature is reached increases toughness and dryness of the cake. At a relatively low temperature, baking beyond the optimum time is less serious than at a relatively high temperature.

OBJECTIVES

1. To understand the factors contributing to albumen foam volumes.
2. To understand the factors contributing to albumen foam stability.
3. To demonstrate an understanding of each of the product formulation ingredients and their contribution to the sensory attributes (color, flavor, texture) of the angel cake product.
4. To explain how foam formation occurs.
5. To explain the role of physical manipulation of the flour–sucrose mixture and beating of egg albumen on the sensory attributes of the angel cake product.
6. To understand the influence of baking conditions in determining product quality.
7. To contrast the merits of using various sucrose concentrations, flour concentrations, and flour types on angel cake quality.

MATERIALS

flour, all-purpose	$1/4$ lb
flour, cake	1 lb
sucrose, white granulated	3 lb
eggs, fresh	$3 1/2$ doz
cream of tartar (tartaric acid)	1 oz

cornstarch	$^1/_4$ cup
sodium chloride (salt)	$^1/_4$ cup
loaf pans, small, 3 × 6 in.	18
electric mixers, hand	18
waxed paper	1 roll
plastic wrap	1 roll
volumeter	1
rubber spatulas	18
bowls, mixing, medium size	18
bowls, mixing, small size	18
flour sifters	18
cooling racks	10
custard cups	36

PRODUCT FORMULATION (BASIC)

flour, cake	15 g
sucrose	42 g
egg albumen	41 g
tartaric acid	0.6 g
sodium chloride	0.1 g

PROCEDURES (BASIC)

1. Weigh or measure all of the ingredients using top-loading balances and/ or graduated cylinders. The sucrose should be weighed out into two quantities: 10 g and 32 g.
2. Preheat oven to 177°C (350°F).
3. Line the bottom of one *ungreased* loaf pan with waxed paper. Cut the paper to just fit the bottom of the pan.
4. Sift the flour and 10 g sucrose together into a small bowl. Set aside.
5. In a medium-sized mixing bowl, beat the egg whites for 1 min using an electric mixer on medium speed.
6. Add the tartaric acid and sodium chloride. Beat 1 min on medium speed.
7. Now, beat the foam on high speed while gradually incorporating 32 g sucrose into the mixture. Add the sucrose in three equal increments, beating enough to blend (10 sec) between additions.
8. Beat the egg whites until the peaks just bend over.
9. Spoon one-quarter of the flour–sucrose mixture over the meringue.
10. Gently fold the flour–sucrose mixture into the egg whites using 10 strokes with a rubber spatula. Repeat three more times until all of the flour–sucrose mixture is incorporated into the foam.

11. Fold an extra 10 strokes to completely blend the mixture. (This will make a total of 50 strokes).
12. Gently pour the batter into the lined loaf pan. If the oven is to be shared by more than one product, put the cakes into the oven at the same time.
13. Bake at 177°C (350°F) for approximately 30 min or until the surface springs back when lightly touched.
14. Cool in an inverted position on a wire rack for 15 min. If the cake rises higher than the sides of the container, suspend the inverted pan between two custard cups.
15. Remove the product (and waxed paper) and perform the objective and sensory assessments.

VARIABLES

1. Flour/sucrose incorporation (follow the basic procedures, except as directed)
   (a) *50 strokes (control)*. Prepare the basic product formulation.
   (b) *20 strokes*. Prepare the basic product formulation. Fold 5 strokes after each one-quarter addition of the flour–sucrose mixture instead of 10 strokes. Delete the extra 10 strokes. There will be a total of 20 strokes in the folding process.
   (c) *80 strokes*. Prepare the basic product formulation. Fold 20 strokes after each one-quarter addition of the flour–sucrose mixture instead of 10 strokes. Delete the extra 10 strokes. There will be a total of 80 strokes in the folding process.
   (d) *120 strokes*. Prepare the basic product formulation. Fold 30 strokes after each one-quarter addition of the flour–sucrose mixture instead of 10 strokes. Delete the extra 10 strokes. There will be a total of 120 strokes in the folding process.
2. Time (follow the basic procedures, except as directed)
   (a) *Underbeating*. Prepare the basic product formulation. Beat the egg whites only to the point where they will not quite hold a peak instead of beating the egg whites until the peaks just bend over.
   (b) *Overbeating*. Prepare the basic product formulation. Beat the egg whites until brittle and dry instead of beating the egg whites until the peaks just bend over.
3. Acid (for all types follow the basic procedures)
   (a) *0 g tartaric acid*. Prepare the basic product formulation but omit the tartaric acid. The basic procedures are to be followed.
   (b) *0.6 g tartaric acid (control)*. Prepare the basic product formulation.
   (c) *0.9 g tartaric acid*. Prepare the basic product formulation but use 0.9 g tartaric acid instead of 0.6 g tartaric acid.

   (d) **1.2 g tartaric acid.** Prepare the basic product formulation but use 1.2 g tartaric acid instead of 0.6 g tartaric acid.

4. Flour types/concentrations (for all types follow the basic procedures)

   (a) **Flour, all-purpose.** Prepare the basic product formulation but use 15 g all-purpose flour instead of 15 g cake flour.

   (b) **Cornstarch.** Prepare the basic product formulation but use 15 g cornstarch instead of 15 g cake flour.

   (c) **10 g flour, cake** (67%). Prepare the basic product formulation but use 10 g cake flour instead of 15 g cake flour.

   (d) **20 g flour, cake** (133%). Prepare the basic product formulation but use 20 g cake flour instead of 15 g cake flour.

5. Sucrose concentrations (for all types follow the basic procedures)

   (a) **34 g sucrose** (80%). Prepare the basic product formulation. Use 8 g sucrose instead of 10 g sucrose in the flour–sugar mixture, and use 26 g sucrose instead of 32 g sucrose during foam formation.

   (b) **42 g sucrose (control).** Prepare the basic product formulation.

   (c) **51 g sucrose** (120%). Prepare the basic product formulation. Use 13 g sucrose instead of 10 g sucrose in the flour–sugar mixture, and use 38 g sucrose instead of 32 g sucrose during foam formation.

   (d) **67 g sucrose** (160%). Prepare the basic product formulation. Use 17 g sucrose instead of 10 g sucrose in the flour–sugar mixture, and use 50 g sucrose instead of 32 g sucrose during foam formation.

ASSESSMENT

Objective Measurements

Volumeter
Wrap the loaf in plastic wrap. Place the product in the volumeter and find the volume of the product by subtracting the volume of the rapeseeds of the empty container from the volume of the rapeseeds that are surrounding the product. Repeat the measurement on the same loaf and record the values and the average value on the protein-foams data sheet.

Subjective Measurements

Acceptance/Preference
Evaluate each product in terms of how much you *like* or *dislike* the sample you have tasted based on the Food Attitude Rating Form (FACT) (Table 13.1). Record your response for each product on the protein-foams data sheet.

Table 13.1. Food Attitude Rating Form for FACT Method

I would eat this every opportunity I had. _____
I would eat this very often. _____
I would frequently eat this. _____
I like this and would eat it now and then. _____
I would eat this if available but would not go out of my way. _____
I don't like it but would eat it on occasion. _____
I would hardly ever eat this. _____
I would eat this only if there were no other food choices. _____
I would eat this if I were forced to. _____

SOURCE: Campbell, A. M., Penfield, M. P., and Griswold, R. M. 1979. *The Experimental Study of Food*, chapter 15, p. 446. Houghton Mifflin Co., Boston. Reprinted with permission.

STUDY QUESTIONS

1. Define foam.
2. What effect can be noted as the amount of mixing is increased in folding the flour–sucrose mixture into the egg white foam? Why would one predict this effect?
3. What factors are involved in contributing to albumen-foam volumes?
4. What factors are involved in contributing to albumen-foam stability?
5. What is the functional role of each of the ingredients in the angel cake formulation?
6. Explain the formation of a foam.
7. Compare the characteristics of angel cakes made with albumen that are (a) underbeaten, (b) beaten correctly, (c) overbeaten. Why are there differences?
8. Describe the changes that can be noted when the level of tartaric acid varies from none to twice the required amount. Why does cake color change when tartaric acid is used?
9. What is the effect of (a) reducing the amount of cake flour, (b) increasing the amount of cake flour, (c) substituting all-purpose flour? Why?
10. What is the effect of using various sucrose concentrations on angel cake product quality? Why?

SELECTED BIBLIOGRAPHY

Baldwin, R. E. 1973. Functional properties in foods. In *Egg Science and Technology*, Stadelman, W. J. and Cotterill, O. J. (Eds.). AVI Publishing, Westport, CT.
Baldwin, R. E., Upchurch, R., and Cotterill, O. J. 1968. Ingredient effects on meringues cooked by microwaves and by baking. *Food Technol.* 22:1573.
Barmore, M. A. 1934. *The Influence of Chemical and Physical Factors on Egg-White Foams*. Tech. Bull. 9, Colorado Agric. Exp. Stn., Fort Collins, CO.

Campbell, A. M., Penfield, M. P., and Griswold, R. M. 1979. *The Experimental Study of Food*, chapter 3. Houghton Mifflin Co., Boston.

Charley, H. 1982. *Food Science*, chapters 19, 20. John Wiley & Sons, New York.

Clinger, C., Young, A., Prudent, I., and Winter, A. R. 1951. The influence of pasteurization, freezing, and storage on the functional properties of egg white. *Food Technol.* 5:166.

Cunningham, F. E. and Cotterill, O. J. 1972. Performance of egg white in the presence of yolk fractions. *Poultry Sci.* 51:712.

Eisen, E. J. and Bohren, B. B. 1963. Some problems in the evaluation of egg albumen quality. *Poultry Sci.* 43: 74.

Elgidaily, D. A., Funk, K. and Zabik, M. E. 1969. Baking temperature and quality of angel cakes. *J. Am. Dietet. Assoc.* 54:401.

Felt, S. A., Longree, K., and Briant, A. M. 1956. Instability of meringued pies. *J. Am. Dietet. Assoc.* 32:710.

Forsythe, R. H. and Bergquist, D. H. 1951. The effect of physical treatments on some properties of egg whites. *Poultry Sci.* 30:302.

Franks, O. J., Zabik, M. E., and Funk, K. 1969. Angel cakes using frozen, foam-spray-dried, freeze-dried, and spray-dried albumen. *Cereal Chem.* 46:349.

Gillis, J. N. and Fitch, N. K. 1956. Leakage of baked soft-meringue topping. *J. Home Econ.* 48:703.

Hanning, F. M. 1945. Effect of sugar or salt upon denaturation produced by beating and upon the ease of formation and the stability of egg white foams. *Iowa State College J. Sci.* 20:10.

MacDonald, L. R., Feeney, R. E., Hanson, H. L., Campbell, A., and Sugihara, T. F. 1955. The functional properties of the egg white proteins. *Food Technol.* 9:49.

McKellar, D. M. B. and Stadelman, W. J. 1955. A method for measuring volume and drainage of egg white foams. *Poultry Sci.* 34:455.

Miller, E. L. and Vail, G. E. 1943. Angel food cakes made from fresh and frozen egg whites. *Cereal Chem.* 20:528.

Paul, P. C. and Palmer, H. H. 1972. *Food Theory and Applications*, chapters 3, 9. John Wiley & Sons, New York.

Powrie, W. D. 1973. Chemistry of eggs and egg products. In *Egg Science and Technology*, Stadelman, W. J. and Cotterill, O. J. (Eds.). AVI Publishing, Westport, CT.

Reinke, W. C., Spencer, J. V., and Tryhnew, L. J. 1973. The effect of storage upon the chemical, physical, and functional properties of chicken eggs. *Poultry Sci.* 52:692.

Sauter, E. A. and Montroure, J. E. 1972. The relationship of lysozyme content of egg white to volume and stability of foams. *J. Food Sci.* 37:918.

DATA SHEET
PROTEIN FOAMS

NAME _____

DATE _____

VARIABLES	VOLUME (cm³)			FACT RESPONSE
	Reading No. 1	Reading No. 2	Average	
Flour/Sucrose Incorporation 50 strokes (control)				
20 strokes				
80 strokes				
120 strokes				
Time Underbeating				
Overbeating				
Acid 0 g tartaric acid				
0.6 g tartaric acid (control)				
0.9 g tartaric acid				
1.2 g tartaric acid				
Flour types/concentrations Flour, all-purpose				
Cornstarch				
10 g flour, cake (67%)				
20 g flour, cake (133%)				
Sucrose concentrations 34 g sucrose (80%)				
42 g sucrose (control)				
51 g sucrose (120%)				
67 g sucrose (160%)				

Chapter 14

Experiment: Soy Protein Extenders

THEORY

Technological advances have made it possible to have soybean protein available in various forms: as whole seeds and flours, protein concentrates, and protein isolates. These products differ in functional properties as well as in fat and protein content; however, amino acid patterns on a protein basis are essentially the same. Nutritionally, these products have in common a highly digestible protein with ample amounts of lysine and a relatively good essential amino acid pattern. Soybeans have contributed to food systems as sources of calories, as supplementary protein, and as complementary protein because of their good essential amino acid pattern. Furthermore, soybean protein products have made significant contributions to food systems because of their functional properties, which are essential in order to derive benefit from the nutritional or economic enhancement they impart to other foods. Many examples of this are found in the literature and in practice. Whole soybeans have been used to extend common beans, providing higher energy concentration and higher protein content and quality. Full-fat flour or protein concentrates added in variable amounts to cereal-grain flours have introduced higher energy and higher protein content and quality into foods based on maize, rice, or wheat. Finally, the amino acid pattern of soybean protein products has allowed them to be used as extenders for cow's milk and meat products, without altering the protein quality or acceptability of the food product.

Basic Principles of Utilization

Two basic categories of soy protein utilization are (a) in traditional foods or (b) in new foods. The success of soy proteins in traditional foods is based on reformulating traditional products in such a manner that the traditional quality of the product is maintained. In new foods, where quality standards may not have been established, soy products must also contribute to the overall appeal of the products.

The world's food supply is composed primarily of traditional foods, defined as those that have been used by the consumer long enough to have an established standard of quality. Products purchased as traditional foods that do not deliver the anticipated quality are commercially unsuccessful. Soy products have been the most successful in traditional products as partial replacement of animal proteins when the traditional food characteristics and quality are unchanged. A portion of the animal proteins can be replaced or extended with soy proteins while maintaining traditional quality. In addition to extending the supply of meat, poultry, or fish proteins, the unit cost of the food will be lower. As opposed to a complete replacement, partially replaced meat, fish, and poultry products more successfully compare to the traditional counterparts, thus allowing for the continuation of basic consumption patterns.

To be successful, traditional products must be reformulated with soy proteins so that the traditional quality is maintained. This means identical color, flavor, texture, odor, overall eating quality, nutrition, and chemical composition.

Soybean Products

The numbers and types of soy products have increased appreciably in the past several years. However, basic product grouping may be classified as shown in Table 14.1. From these main products, using particular technologies, other soybean foods have been prepared, including textured vegetable proteins, expanded or compacted with 50–53% protein; spun-fiber textured products; and other soy food products, such as milk and cheese, Oriental foods, and hydrolyzed products.

Table 14.1. Typical Chemical Composition of Soy Protein Products (g/100 g)

PRODUCT	PROTEIN	FAT	FIBER	ASH	CHO
Whole soybean	41.0	20.0	2.3	5.4	31.3
Soy flours	50.0	1.0	3.5	6.0	39.5
Concentrates	70.0	1.0	4.5	5.0	19.5
Isolates	96.0	0.1	0.1	3.5	0.3

SOURCE: Bressani, R. 1981. The role of soybeans in food systems. *J. Am. Oil Chemists' Soc.* 58:393. Reprinted with permission of the American Oil Chemists' Society.

Functional Properties

One of the significant attributes of soybean protein is that, by controlling processing conditions, soybean products can be made with different functional properties that are useful in a variety of food systems and applications. These functional properties have been well described and are shown in Table 14.2. These properties are generally attributed to the protein; however, other chemical components in some products may also participate in imparting functional characteristics. For example, polysaccharides in soybean flour and grits will absorb more water than an equivalent amount of protein.

Meat Systems

A major application of soy protein products is in meats, for which experience has shown that traditional quality must be maintained for consumer acceptance.

The two principal forms of consumed meat are the intact muscle and comminuted products. Soy protein products are being used in each form. Comminuted products were one of the first meat applications of soy protein products. Emulsified meats (frankfurters) and coarse ground meats (ground-beef patties) are two important classes of comminuted products. In emulsified meats, the nonmeat proteins must perform the same functions as the salt-soluble meat proteins. These functions include emulsification, gelation, and fat and water binding. Depending on the protein ingredient used and the meat product, levels of usage range from 1 to 4% in emulsified meat products. In coarse-ground meats, texture-contributing properties are particularly important.

For any specific soy product, a maximal level of meat replacement is achieved beyond which reformulations to improve color, texture, and flavor do not maintain traditional quality. Under these conditions, an improved soy protein product is required to increase the level of meat replacement. It would be a major error to conclude that all soy products are alike. Soy ingredient manufacturers are continually conducting research to develop products with improved meat-replacement capabilities.

Ground beef is a coarse-ground, comminuted product that also serves as an example of how a traditional product has been reformulated with soy proteins. Again, there are differences between soy products in this application, and the levels of successful replacement vary from one soy ingredient to the next. Textured vegetable proteins (TVPs) have been used to extend ground meat as a means of reducing cost without reducing nutritional value (Lachance, 1972). Federal school-lunch regulations allow for inclusion of up

Table 14.2. Functional Properties of Soy Protein Preparation in Food Systems

FUNCTIONAL PROPERTIES	MODE OF ACTION	FOOD SYSTEM	PREPARATION USED*
Solubility	Protein solvation, pH dependent	beverages	F, C, I, H
Water absorption & binding	Hydrogen bonding of HOH Entrapment of HOH, no drip	meats, sausages, bologna, bread, cakes	F, C
Viscosity	Thickening, HOH binding	soups, gravies	F, C, I
Gelation	Protein matrix formation and setting	meats, curds, cheese	C, I
Cohesion/ adhesion	Protein acts as adhesive material	meats, sausages, baked goods, pasta products	F, C, I
Elasticity	Disulfide links in gels, deformable	meats, baked goods	I
Emulsification	Formation and stabilization of fat emulsions	sausages, bologna, soup, cakes	F, C, I
Fat adsorption	Binding of free fat	meats, sausages, doughnuts	F, C, I
Flavor binding	Adsorption, entrapment	simulated meats, bakery goods	C, I, H
Foaming	Forms stable films to entrap gas	whipped toppings, chiffon desserts, angel cakes	I, W, H
Color control	Bleaching of lipoxygenase	breads	F

SOURCE: Bressani, R. 1981. The role of soybeans in food systems. *J. Am. Oil Chemists' Soc.* **58**:393. Reprinted with permission of the American Oil Chemists' Society.
*F, C, I, H, and W denote soy flour, concentrate, isolate, hydrolyzate, and whey, respectively.

to 30% of TVP in ground meat for that program (USDA, 1971). Addition of TVP influences the quality of ground-meat products, as indicated in several studies. The effect on quality depends on the level of TVP added. Textured soy protein (TSP) products have been used as the extender in most studies.

Anderson and Lind (1975) reported that beef patties containing 25% TVP retained more moisture and less fat than beef patties with comparable initial fat content. Similar results were reported by Seideman et al. (1977). However, these workers also reported that flavor desirability and overall palatability decreases as the level of TSP increased to 20 to 30%. The authors concluded that 10% TSP can be added without significantly affecting cooked appearance and palatability. Increased moisture content in extended patties does not increase panel scores for juiciness (Bowers and Engler, 1975). Patties containing 20% TVP were reported to be as acceptable as all-beef patties by Cross et al. (1975). Turkey patties containing 10% TSP were as acceptable as all-turkey patties, but those containing 20% TSP were not (Baldwin et al., 1975).

Reheating of patties containing TSP and all-meat patties reduced flavor differences (Bowers and Engler, 1975). Stale taste and aroma were almost absent in reheated patties containing soy, suggesting that if components responsible for stale taste and aroma were present, other components masked the stale flavors.

The addition of ingredients such as vinegar, pineapple, horseradish, and soy sauce reduces the undesirable effects of soy proteins on the flavor of combination dishes (Baldwin et al., 1975). Cooking method also may influence quality of soy and beef products. Microwave heating of beef–soy loaves resulted in increased loss of moisture and reduced beef flavor (Ziprin and Carlin, 1976).

OBJECTIVES

1. To understand the functional properties of soy proteins.
2. To be aware of the potential for using soy protein extenders in food systems.
3. To determine the optimum percentage of soy protein extender to be used in a ground-beef system in order to maintain product quality.
4. To become knowledgeable of the benefits and limitations of using textured soy protein in ground-beef formulations.
5. To understand how soy proteins can influence water-binding capacity, and lipid, volatile, and total cooking losses in a ground-beef system.
6. To understand the effect of increasing levels of soy protein on product acceptability.
7. To determine whether there is a relationship between the percentage press fluid loss and the soy protein concentration in the product.
8. To learn to calculate cooking losses in meat products.

MATERIALS

textured soy protein, beef flavored, granules	2 lb
textured soy protein, ham flavored, granules	2 lb
textured soy protein, chicken flavored, granules	2 lb
beef, ground	11 lb
eggs, fresh	$1^{1}/_{2}$ doz
onions, white fresh	4 large
sodium chloride (salt)	$^{1}/_{2}$ cup
laboratory thermometers	18
Carver press	1
loaf pans, 3×6 in.	18
bowls, medium size	18
bowls, mixing, large size	18
electric mixers, hand	18
cooling racks	10
graduated cylinders, 50 ml or 100 ml	18
strainers	18

PRODUCT FORMULATION (BASIC)

beef, ground	454 g
egg, whole	48 g
onion, chopped	45 g
sodium chloride	2.5 g

PROCEDURES (BASIC)

1. Weigh or measure all the ingredients using top-loading balances and/or graduated cylinders.
2. Weigh the empty loaf container. Record data on the soy-protein-calculations data sheet.
3. Calibrate thermometers. Adjust procedure temperatures accordingly.
4. Preheat an oven to 177°C (350°F).
5. In a large mixing bowl, thoroughly blend the product formulation ingredients together using an electric mixer on slow speed for 1 min.
6. Shape the mixture into a small loaf pan.
7. Weigh the filled loaf container. Record data on the soy-protein-calculations data sheet.
8. Insert a thermometer so that the bulb is in the center of the raw product. Use an oven rack positioned above the meat product to support the thermometer during the heating process.
9. Bake at 177°C (350°F) to an internal temperature of 77°C (170°F). This will take approximately 50–60 min. Note and record the total

baking time required to reach the final interior temperature on the calculations data sheet.

10. Remove the sample from the oven when the specified internal temperature has been reached. Remove the thermometer.

11. Place the product on a cooling rack and cool uncovered at ambient temperature for 5 min.

12. Weigh the baked product before removal from the container. Record data on the soy-protein-calculations data sheet.

13. Carefully remove the meat product from the loaf container. Weigh the loaf container with the drippings remaining in the loaf pan. Record data on the soy-protein-calculations data sheet.

14. Pour the drippings into a 50 ml or 100 ml graduated cylinder and note the milliliters of lipid lost from the product. This may be seen after the lipid has risen to the top of the cylinder. Record the data on the soy-protein-calculations data sheet.

15. Conduct the objective and sensory assessments. Calculate cooking losses.

VARIABLES

1. TSP—beef flavored (for all types follow the basic procedures)

   (a) *0% TSP beef flavored (control)*. Prepare the basic product formulation.

   (b) *15% TSP, beef flavored*. Reconstitute 34 g beef-flavored TSP with 102 ml of 100°C (212°F) water. Allow the TSP to absorb the water for 15 min before proceeding with the formulation. Drain excess water from the TSP using a strainer. Prepare the basic product formulation but use 68 g reconstituted beef-flavored TSP plus 386 g ground beef instead of 454 g ground beef.

   (c) *30% TSP, beef flavored*. Reconstitute 68 g beef-flavored TSP with 204 ml of 100°C (212°F) water. Allow the TSP to absorb the water for 15 min before proceeding with the formulation. Drain excess water from the TSP using a strainer. Prepare the basic product formulation but use 136 g reconstituted beef-flavored TSP plus 318 g ground beef instead of 454 g ground beef.

   (d) *45% TSP, beef flavored*. Reconstitute 102 g beef-flavored TSP with 306 ml of 100°C (212°F) water. Allow the TSP to absorb the water for 15 min before proceeding with the formulation. Drain excess water from the TSP using a strainer. Prepare the basic product formulation but use 204 g reconstituted beef-flavored TSP plus 250 g ground beef instead of 454 g ground beef.

   (e) *60% TSP, beef flavored*. Reconstitute 136 g beef-flavored TSP with 408 ml of 100°C (212°F) water. Allow the TSP to absorb the water for 15 min before proceeding with the formulation. Drain excess water from the TSP using a strainer. Prepare the basic product formulation but use 272 g reconstituted beef-flavored TSP plus 182 g ground beef instead of 454 g ground beef.

(f) *75% TSP, beef flavored*. Reconstitute 170 g beef-flavored TSP with 512 ml of 100°C (212°F) water. Allow the TSP to absorb the water for 15 min before proceeding with the formulation. Drain excess water from the TSP using a strainer. Prepare the basic product formulation but use 341 g reconstituted beef-flavored TSP plus 113 g ground beef instead of 454 g ground beef.

(g) *100% TSP, beef flavored*. Reconstitute 227 g beef-flavored TSP with 682 ml of 100°C (212°F) water. Allow the TSP to absorb the water for 15 min before proceeding with the formulation. Drain excess water from the TSP using a strainer. Prepare the basic product formulation but use 454 g reconstituted beef-flavored TSP instead of 454 g ground beef.

2. TSP—ham flavored (for all types follow the basic procedures)

(a) *15% TSP, ham flavored*. Reconstitute 34 g ham-flavored TSP with 102 ml of 100°C (212°F) water. Allow the TSP to absorb the water for 15 min before proceeding with the formulation. Drain excess water from the TSP using a strainer. Prepare the basic product formulation but use 68 g reconstituted ham-flavored TSP plus 386 g ground beef instead of 454 g ground beef.

(b) *30% TSP, ham flavored*. Reconstitute 68 g ham-flavored TSP with 204 ml of 100°C (212°F) water. Allow the TSP to absorb the water for 15 min before proceeding with the formulation. Drain excess water from the TSP using a strainer. Prepare the basic product formulation but use 136 g reconstituted ham-flavored TSP plus 318 g ground beef instead of 454 g ground beef.

(c) *45% TSP, ham flavored*. Reconstitute 102 g ham-flavored TSP with 306 ml of 100°C (212°F) water. Allow the TSP to absorb the water for 15 min before proceeding with the formulation. Drain excess water from the TSP using a strainer. Prepare the basic product formulation but use 204 g reconstituted ham-flavored TSP plus 250 g ground beef instead of 454 g ground beef.

(d) *60% TSP, ham flavored*. Reconstitute 136 g ham-flavored TSP with 408 ml of 100°C (212°F) water. Allow the TSP to absorb the water for 15 min before proceeding with the formulation. Drain excess water from the TSP using a strainer. Prepare the basic product formulation but use 272 g reconstituted ham-flavored TSP plus 182 g ground beef instead of 454 g ground beef.

(e) *75% TSP, ham flavored*. Reconstitute 170 g ham-flavored TSP with 512 ml of 100°C (212°F) water. Allow the TSP to absorb the water for 15 min before proceeding with the formulation. Drain excess water from the TSP using a strainer. Prepare the basic product formulation but use 341 g reconstituted ham-flavored TSP plus 113 g ground beef instead of 454 g ground beef.

(f) **100% TSP, ham flavored.** Reconstitute 227 g ham-flavored TSP with 682 ml of 100°C (212°F) water. Allow the TSP to absorb the water for 15 min before proceeding with the formulation. Drain excess water from the TSP using a strainer. Prepare the basic product formulation but use 454 g reconstituted ham-flavored TSP instead of 454 g ground beef.

3. TSP—chicken flavored (for all types follow the basic procedures)

(a) **15% TSP, chicken flavored.** Reconstitute 34 g chicken-flavored TSP with 102 ml of 100°C (212°F) water. Allow the TSP to absorb the water for 15 min before proceeding with the formulation. Drain excess water from the TSP using a strainer. Prepare the basic product formulation but use 68 g reconstituted chicken-flavored TSP plus 386 g ground beef instead of 454 g ground beef.

(b) **30% TSP, chicken flavored.** Reconstitute 68 g chicken-flavored TSP with 204 ml of 100°C (212°F) water. Allow the TSP to absorb the water for 15 min before proceeding with the formulation. Drain excess water from the TSP using a strainer. Prepare the basic product formulation but use 136 g reconstituted chicken-flavored TSP plus 318 g ground beef instead of 454 g ground beef.

(c) **45% TSP, chicken flavored.** Reconstitute 102 g chicken-flavored TSP with 306 ml of 100°C (212°F) water. Allow the TSP to absorb the water for 15 min before proceeding with the formulation. Drain excess water from the TSP using a strainer. Prepare the basic product formulation but use 204 g reconstituted chicken-flavored TSP plus 250 g ground beef instead of 454 g ground beef.

(d) **60% TSP, chicken flavored.** Reconstitute 136 g chicken-flavored TSP with 408 ml of 100°C (212°F) water. Allow the TSP to absorb the water for 15 min before proceeding with the formulation. Drain excess water from the TSP using a strainer. Prepare the basic product formulation but use 272 g reconstituted chicken-flavored TSP plus 182 g ground beef instead of 454 g ground beef.

(e) **75% TSP, chicken flavored.** Reconstitute 170 g chicken-flavored TSP with 512 ml of 100°C (212°F) water. Allow the TSP to absorb the water for 15 min before proceeding with the formulation. Drain excess water from the TSP using a strainer. Prepare the basic product formulation but use 341 g reconstituted chicken-flavored TSP plus 113 g ground beef instead of 454 g ground beef.

(f) **100% TSP, chicken flavored.** Reconstitute 227 g chicken-flavored TSP with 682 ml of 100°C (212°F) water. Allow the TSP to absorb the water for 15 min before proceeding with the formulation. Drain excess water from the TSP using a strainer. Prepare the basic product formulation but use 454 g reconstituted chicken-flavored TSP instead of 454 g ground beef.

ASSESSMENT

Objective Measurements

Carver Press
Extract a 2 g meat sample from the center of the product. Place sample at the center of a 3 in. canvas pad and cover with a second canvas pad. Place this assembly first between two felt pads and then between two metal discs. Pump the press to 15,000 lb/sq in. and hold this pressure for 3 min. Remove the sample from the Carver press and carefully scrape it from the canvas pad onto the preweighed weighing paper. Reweigh the sample and calculate the percentage of press fluid. Percentage press fluid is calculated by this formula:

$$\% \text{ press fluid} = \frac{\text{original wt. (g)} - \text{pressed wt. (g)}}{\text{original wt. (g)}} \times 100.$$

Record the data on the soy-protein-calculations data sheet.

Cooking Loss Calculations
Record these data on the soy-protein-calculations data sheet.

1. Volatile

$$\text{Volatile loss (g)} = (\text{wt. of pan} + \text{raw product}) - (\text{wt. of pan} + \text{cooked product} + \text{drippings}).$$

$$\% \text{ Volatile loss} = \frac{\text{volatile loss (g)}}{\text{wt. raw product (g)}} \times 100.$$

2. Drip

$$\text{Drip loss (g)} = (\text{wt. of pan} + \text{drippings}) - (\text{wt. of pan}).$$

$$\% \text{ Drip loss} = \frac{\text{drip loss (g)}}{\text{wt. raw product (g)}} \times 100.$$

3. Total cooking

$$\text{Total cooking loss (g)} = \text{volatile loss} + \text{drip loss}.$$

$$\% \text{ Cooking loss} = \frac{\text{wt. raw product (g)} - \text{wt. cooked product (g)}}{\text{wt. raw product (g)}} \times 100.$$

4. Lipid

Lipid loss (ml) = amount measured in graduated cylinder.

5. Cooking time

$$\text{Cooking Time (min/g)} = \frac{\text{total cooking time}}{\text{wt. raw product (g)}} .$$

Subjective Measurements

Acceptance/Preference

Evaluate each product in terms of how much you *like* or *dislike* the sample you have tasted. Use the following hedonic scale. Keep in mind that you are the judge. You are the only one who can tell what you like. Nobody knows whether this product should be considered good, bad, or indifferent. An honest expression of your personal feeling will help us to decide.

_____ like extremely (7)
_____ like moderately (6)
_____ like slightly (5)
_____ neither like/dislike (4)
_____ dislike slightly (3)
_____ dislike moderately (2)
_____ dislike extremely (1)

Record your response on the soy-protein-extender data sheet.

STUDY QUESTIONS

1. What is the effect of increasing levels of TSP in terms of product acceptability, volatile losses, drip losses, total cooking losses, lipid losses, cooking time, and percentage press fluid?
2. At what maximum level would it be acceptable from a sensory standpoint to incorporate TSP into ground-meat products?
3. Identify the advantages and disadvantages of using TSP at various levels in ground-meat products considering functional, sensory, and nutritional attributes of TSP.
4. Cite the functional properties of soy proteins.

SELECTED BIBLIOGRAPHY

Ali, F. S., Perry, A. K., and Van Duyne, F. O. 1982. Soybeans versus textured soy protein as meat extenders. *J. Am. Dietet. Assn.* **81**:439.

Anderson, R. H. and Lind, K. D. 1975. Retention of water and fat in cooked patties of beef and of beef extended with textured vegetable protein. *Food Tech.* **25**:44.

Baldwin, R. E., Korschgen, B. M., Vandepopuliere, J. M., and Russell, W. D. 1975. Palatability of ground turkey and beef containing soy. *Poultry Sci.* **54**:1102.

Bowers, J. A. and Engler, P. P. 1975. Freshly cooked and cooked, frozen, reheated beef and beef–soy patties. *J. Food Sci.* **40**:624.

Bressani, R. 1981. The role of soybeans in food systems. *J. Am. Oil Chemists' Soc.* **58**:393.

Carlin, F., Ziprin, Y., Zabik, M. E., Kraft, L., Polsiri, A., Bowers, J., Rainey, B., VanDuyne, F., and Perry, A. K. 1978. Texturized soy protein in beef loaves: Cooking losses, flavor, juiciness, and chemical composition. *J. Food Sci.* **43**:830.

Cross, H. R., Stanfield, M. S., Green, E. C., Heinemeyer, J. M., and Hollick, A. B. 1975. Effect of fat and textured soy protein content on consumer acceptance of ground beef. *J. Food Sci.* **40**:1331.

Drake, S. R., Hinnergardt, L. C., Kluter, R. A., and Prell, P. A. 1975. Beef patties: The effect of textured soy protein and fat levels on quality and acceptability. *J. Food Sci.* **40**:1065.

Lachance, P. A. 1972. Update: Meat extenders and analogues in child feeding programs. *Proc. Meat Ind. Res. Conf.* **24**:97.

Meyer, L. H. 1982. *Food Chemistry*, chapter 6. AVI Publishing, Westport, CT.

Seideman, S. C., Smith, G. C., and Carpenter, Z. L. 1977. Addition of textured soy protein and mechanically deboned beef to ground beef formulations. *J. Food Sci.* **42**:197.

Shaner, K. M. and Baldwin, R. E. 1979. Sensory properties, proximate analysis, and cooking losses of meat loaves extended with chickpea meal or textured soy protein. *J. Food Sci.* **44**:1191.

USDA. 1971. *Textured Vegetable Protein Products* (B-1). Notice 219, Food and Nutrition Service, USDA, Washington, DC.

Williams, C. W. and Zabik, M. E. 1975. Quality characteristics of soy-substituted ground beef, pork, and turkey meat loaves. *J. Food Sci.* **40**:502.

Wolf, W. J. 1970. Soybean proteins: Their functional, chemical and physical properties. *J. Agr. Food Chem.* **18**:969.

Ziprin, Y. A. and Carlin, A. F. 1976. Microwave and conventional cooking in relation to quality and nutritive value of beef and beef–soy loaves. *J. Food Sci.* **41**:4.

DATA SHEET
CALCULATIONS FOR SOY PROTEIN EXTENDERS

NAME _____

DATE _____

Cooking data and results for variable: _____

FACTOR MEASURED

Before heat treatment
Wt. of loaf pan (g) = _____
Wt. of product (g) = _____
Wt. of filled loaf pan (g) = _____
Heating time
Total cooking time (min) = _____
Cooking time (min/g)* = _____
After heat treatment
Wt. of pan, cooked product and drip (g) = _____
Wt. of pan and drip (g) = _____
Losses
% Pressed fluid* = _____
Volatile loss (g) = _____
% Volatile loss* = _____
Drip loss (g) = _____
% Drip loss* = _____
Total cooking loss (g) = _____
% Cooking loss* = _____
Lipid loss (ml)* = _____

---

*Record the data on the soy-protein-extender data sheet.

DATA SHEET
SOY PROTEIN EXTENDERS

NAME _____
DATE _____

VARIABLES	COOKING TIME (min/g)	% PRESSED FLUID	% VOLATILE LOSS	% DRIP LOSS	% COOKING LOSS	ml LIPID LOSS	ACCEPTANCE PREFERENCE VALUE
TSP—Beef (%) 0 TSP (control)							
15 TSP							
30 TSP							
45 TSP							
60 TSP							
75 TSP							
100 TSP							

TSP—Ham (%)						
15 TSP						
30 TSP						
45 TSP						
60 TSP						
75 TSP						
100 TSP						
TSP—Chicken (%)						
15 TSP						
30 TSP						
45 TSP						
60 TSP						
75 TSP						
100 TSP						

Chapter 15

Experiment: Plant Pigments

THEORY

Fruits and vegetables have special consumer appeal, in part because they contain bright, attractive color pigments. Plant pigments are classified into three main classes: the carotenoids, the chlorophylls, and the flavonoids. The flavonoids are further subdivided into a diverse group that includes the anthocyanins, flavones, flavonols, leucoanthocyanins, and related phenolic compounds. The carotenoids and the chlorophylls are fat soluble and are found in the chromoplasts and chloroplasts, respectively. The water-soluble flavonoids are dissolved in the plant cell sap (a watery substance containing many substances such as sugars, salts, organic acids, polysaccharides, phenolic derivatives, and various pigments).

If fruits and vegetables are improperly handled, these pigments may undergo changes that result in either a less colorful or an unattractive product. In this experiment, we will consider the nature of the pigments and factors affecting pigment changes.

Carotenoids

Color

Carotenoids are yellow, orange, or red pigments so named because the first member of the group was isolated from carrots. In addition to their occurrence as the sole or predominating pigments in some fruits and vegetables, carotenoids always accompany chlorophyll in the ratio of about three or four parts chlorophyll to one part carotenoid. The carotenoids are insoluble in water and soluble in fats and organic solvents. Various members of this large group of related compounds differ in solubility characteristics, offering a convenient method of separating the carotenoids into two groups. The carotenes are hydrocarbons containing only hydrogen and carbon and are soluble in petroleum ether, whereas the xanthophylls are oxygen derivatives of the carotenes and are soluble in alcohol.

Structures

Carotenoids usually contain 40 carbon atoms in configurations such as those for β-carotene, α-carotene, and lycopene shown in Figure 15.1. The commonly occurring carotenoids are composed of eight isoprene residues having a skeleton of 40 carbon atoms that includes an 18-carbon central portion with four methyl groups attached as side chains. Two end groups, either ring structure or open chain, attached to this central portion serve as distinguishing features for individual carotenoids. The carotenoids are polyunsaturated compounds, a number of them with 11 conjugated double bonds as shown for lycopene and β-carotene. Lycopene is an open-chain carotenoid, while β-carotene, the most commonly occurring isomer of the carotenes, has ring closure at either end of the molecule. The conjugated double bonds are responsible for the intense color of foods containing carotenoids. Although many different *cis-* and *trans-* configurations of the structure are possible, most naturally occurring carotenoids appear to have an all *trans*-configuration. As the number of double bonds increases, the hue becomes redder. Lycopene, with two additional double bonds, is redder than β-carotene. These additional double bonds make the difference between the orange color of carrots, in which β-carotene predominates, and the red of

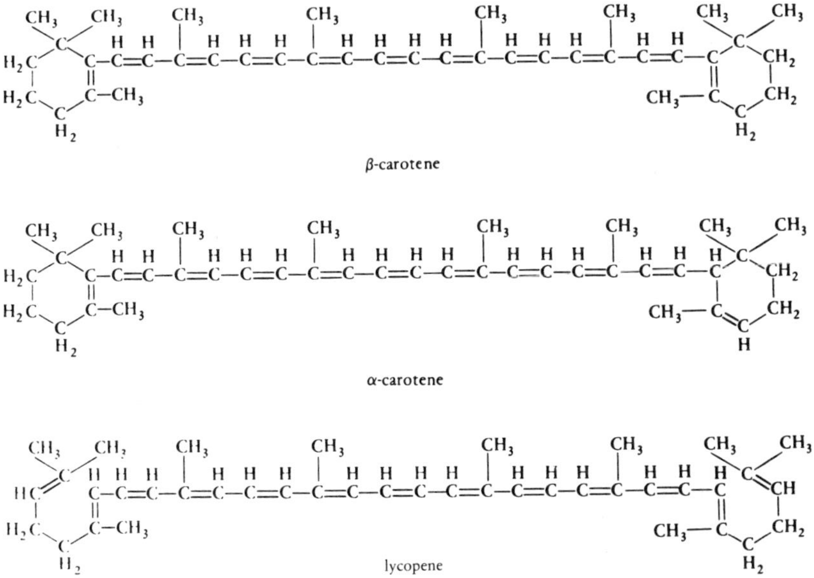

Figure 15.1. Structures of beta-carotene, alpha-carotene, and lycopene. (From Campbell, A. M., Penfield, M. P., and Griswold, R. M. 1979. *The Experimental Study of Food*, chapter 6, p. 176. Houghton Mifflin, Boston. Reprinted with permission.)

tomatoes, in which lycopene is the main carotenoid. A decrease in the number of conjugated double bonds increases yellowness. Consequently, α-carotene is less orange than β-carotene.

Lutein and zeaxanthin are xanthophylls that are similar in structure to α- and β-carotene except for the addition of two hydroxyl groups. Cryptoxanthin contains only one hydroxyl group and is an important pigment in yellow corn, mandarin oranges, and paprika. In addition to their contributions to the appealing colors of fruits and vegetables, most carotenoids are precursors of vitamin A. The symmetrical β-carotene molecule forms two molecules of vitamin A. Carotenoids, such as α- and γ-carotene, in which half of the molecule is exactly like half of the β-carotene molecule, form one molecule of vitamin A. Lycopene has an open-ring structure, rather than the closed-ring one that characterizes β-carotene, and is therefore not a precursor of vitamin A. Most xanthophylls also are not precursors of vitamin A; the exception is cryptoxanthin, which has only one hydroxyl group.

Stability

pH, heating time, temperature. Ordinary cooking methods have little effect on the color or nutritive value of carotenoids. The pigments are little affected by acids, alkalis, the volume of water, or the cooking time. Eheart and Gott (1965) reported complete retention of the carotene in peas heated in water in a conventional oven and with or without water in a microwave oven. Although total carotene content does not change as vegetables are heated in water, there is a shift in the visualized color. For example, the orange of carrots may become yellow and the red of tomatoes may become orange-red. Borchgrevink and Charley (1966) attributed this reduction in color intensity in carrots cooked in several ways to an increase in *cisc*-isomers of β-carotene during cooking. Carrots that appear to be orange-red had a higher concentration of all *trans*-β-carotene than those carrots that appeared yellow. However, Della Monica and McDowell (1965) reported that color changes cannot be explained in terms of isomerization. Shifts in the color of carrots are caused also by the solution of carotene in cellular lipids after release from disintegrated chromoplasts (Purcell et al., 1969). Crystals of lycopene are formed in tomatoes during heating so that shift in color is not as pronounced in tomatoes as in carrots and sweet potatoes. Noble (1975) reported that a conversion of *trans*-lycopene to *cis*-lycopene was not responsible for the loss of redness that occurs as tomato paste is concentrated. This loss was attributed to an actual degradation of lycopene during the extended heating process.

Oxidation. The high degree of unsaturation of the carotenoids makes them susceptible to oxidation, with resulting loss of color, after the food containing them has been dried. Loss of or reduction in color is probably a result of the reaction of peroxides and free radicals, oxidation products of lipids, with the carotenoids (Labuza, 1973). Precooked, dehydrated carrot flakes canned in a nitrogen atmosphere lost little β-carotene, whereas flakes canned in an oxygen atmosphere lost approximately 75% of their β-carotene content (Stephens and McLemore, 1969). Carotene can be protected from oxidation during dehydration by the blanching of vegetables (Dutton et al., 1943) or the sulfuring of fruit.

Chlorophylls

Color
The green pigments of plants, chlorophylls, are found in high concentration in the chloroplasts of the leaf, as well as in other plant parts. These green photosynthetic pigments act as photoreceptors to trap light energy and convert it to chemical energy. Chlorophylls are insoluble in water; thus these pigments cannot be dissolved in plant cell sap or in cooking water. Chlorophylls are soluble in fat and solvents such as ethyl ether, ethanol, acetone, chloroform, carbon disulfide, and benzene.

Structures
The formulas for chlorophylls are shown in Figure 15.2. The structures are similar to that of heme. Both have four pyrrole rings, connected to form a porphyrin nucleus. An atom of magnesium in the center of the molecule is chelated by the four nitrogens of the pyrole groups. Two ester groups, one phytyl and one methyl, are part of the molecule. The presence of the phytyl group is responsible for the insolubility of chlorophyll in water. All higher plants and most lower plants contain two types of chlorophyll, a and b, in the ratio of about three parts of chlorophyll a to one part chlorophyll b. As indicated in Figure 15.2, a formyl group (–CHO) is substituted in chlorophyll b for a methyl group (–CH$_3$) of chlorophyll a. Chlorophyll a is blue–green in color, whereas chlorophyll b is yellow–green. The color of the unsaturated chlorophyll is dependent on the resonance of the conjugated double bonds, of which there are 10.

Stability
When green vegetables are put into boiling water, the immediate effect is an intensification of the color. Expulsion of gas from intercellular spaces, which in the raw vegetable refracts light and dulls the color, is one factor. Change in the condition or distribution of the constituents in the grana has been suggested as another factor. The bright green of the undercooked tissue may in the cooked vegetable become a dull olive green. During cooking, the chloroplasts become shrunken and clumped in the center of a mass of

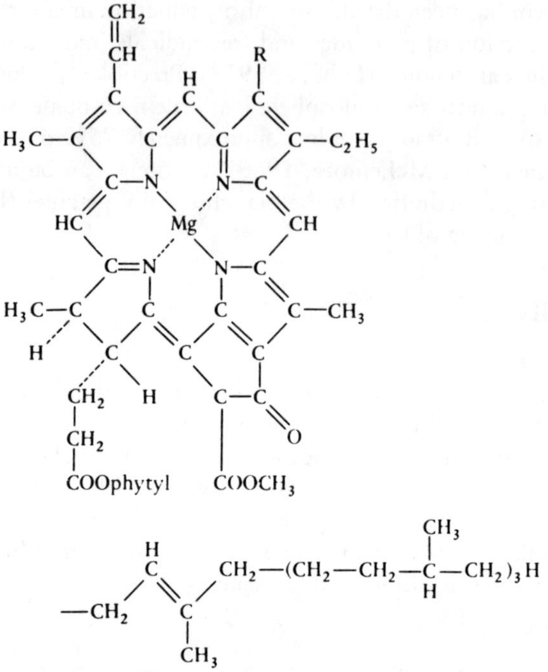

Phytyl group

Figure 15.2. Chlorophyll; in chlorophyll a, R is –CH₃; in chlorophyll b, R is –CHO. (From Campbell, A. M., Penfield, M. P., and Griswold, R. M. 1979. *The Experimental Study of Food*, chapter 6, p. 171. Houghton Mifflin, Boston. Reprinted with permission.)

coagulated protoplasm. The chlorophyll remains in the chloroplasts but is no longer protected by the plastid membranes from the acid-containing cell sap (Mackinney and Weast, 1940). Consequently, the dull olive-green pheophytins may be formed. The speed and extent of change to pheophytins is influenced by several factors, including heating time, pH, temperature, enzymes, and metals.

Heating time. Changes in the chlorophyll molecule that may affect the color include loss of magnesium, removal of phytyl and methyl ester groups, and oxidation of the ring. The length of the heating period influences the alteration of the pigment. Sweeney and Martin (1958) measured loss of chlorophylls a and b when broccoli was cooked for periods of 5, 10, 15, and 20 min. Chlorophyll a was degraded more rapidly than chlorophyll b, to the greater detriment of the color. At the end of 5 min of cooking, retention of chlorophyll a was approximately 80% and of chlorophyll b 90%. At the end of 10 min, retentions were 45% and 87%, respectively. At the end of 20 min less than one-third of the chlorophyll remained, and, what was even worse from the standpoint of color, the ratio of chlorophyll a to chlorophyll b had dropped from 1.77 in broccoli cooked for 5 min to 0.65 in that cooked for 20 min. Mackinney and Joslyn (1940) had reported earlier that chlorophyll a was converted to pheophytin 7 to 9 times faster than was chlorophyll b.

pH. Chlorophylls are sensitive to degradation by acid, particularly by carboxylic acids such as those present in fruits and vegetables. Magnesium in the chlorophyll molecule is displaced and is replaced by two hydrogen atoms. Magnesium-free molecules are referred to as pheophytins; those from chlorophyll a are pheophytin a and those from chlorophyll b are pheophytin b. Pheophytin a is a grayish green and pheophytin b a dull yellowish green. Loss of magnesium from the molecule, especially from chlorophyll a, leads to marked alteration in the color of chlorophyll-rich foods.

The hydrogen-ion concentration of the vegetable influences the speed and extent of conversion of chlorophylls to pheophytins. Sweeney and Martin (1961) reported a high retention of chlorophyll in cooked frozen spinach of 72.2% and in cooked frozen peas of 67.6%, both vegetables having high pH values of 6.8 and 7.0, respectively. Retention in cooked green beans was 26.7% and in brussels sprouts 20.7%, these vegetables having lower pH values of 6.2 and 6.3, respectively. Furthermore, when green beans were cooked in water buffered to elevate the pH, the higher the pH, the better the retention of chlorophyll, up to pH 7. In addition, the higher the pH, the faster the vegetable was tenderized. Cooking green vegetables in a large amount of boiling water to dilute the acid and with the pan uncovered, especially during the first few minutes, to eliminate volatile acids, is a practical technique for minimizing the effects of acid on the color of cooked green vegetables.

Alkaline cooking water will saponify both the phytyl and the methyl ester groups of chlorophyll (Willstatter and Stoll, 1928). The salt of the free carboxylic acid that results, called chlorophyllin, is soluble in water and is a brilliant green color. Vegetables cooked in alkaline water may have a mushy texture because of the breakdown of hemicelluloses.

Metals. Although neither is recommended in foods, copper or zinc ions can replace the displaced magnesium and restore the green color of chlorophyll.

Temperature. The temperature used to blanch green vegetables may affect the conversion of chlorophyll to pheophytin. In one study (Van Buren et al., 1974), in which green beans were held subsequent to blanching, conversion of chlorophyll to pheophytin was greater in those blanched for 2 min at

70°C than in either those unblanched or those blanched at 100°C. The greater conversion of chlorophyll to pheophytin accompanied a decrease in the pH of the beans and a decrease in the water-dispersible pectin. These observations led the authors to suggest that activation of the pectin methylesterase at 70°C and the resulting demethylation of the pectin substances was responsible for the decrease in pH and the greater conversion of chlorophyll to pheophytin.

The effect of blanching on the retention of chlorophyll in green beans during subsequent frozen storage was reported by Walker (1964). Beans were blanched in boiling water for periods of 20, 30, 45, and 60 sec and for 2, 3, 5, and 10 min. Conversion of chlorophylls to pheophytins increased linearly up to 3 min blanching time, after which the conversion leveled off. Blanched beans were held in frozen storage at −10°C for 20 days. Loss of chlorophyll varied with the blanching treatment. Blanching times of 45 sec and 1 min gave best retention of chlorophylls. Loss of chlorophylls in unblanched and in underblanched green beans was attributed in part to conversion of chlorophylls to pheophytins but chiefly to oxidation of chlorophylls as a result of peroxidation of lipids in the beans. The two blanching times that gave the best retentions of chlorophylls were sufficient to completely inactivate both catalase and peroxidase in the green beans. Loss of chlorophylls in overblanched beans was attributed to "heat initiation of other systems," which resulted in oxidation of the chlorophylls. Chapman et al. (1960) compared fresh and frozen broccoli cooked by both microwave and by boiling in a small amount of water. Cooking times for 1 lb of fresh broccoli to achieve optimum tenderness in the stems was 6 min by microwave and 13 min by boiling. Comparable cooking times for 20 oz of frozen broccoli were 13 min by microwave and 11 min by boiling. The color of fresh broccoli cooked electronically was judged slightly better than that cooked by boiling, but the panel ranked frozen broccoli cooked by boiling above that cooked electronically. Gordon and Noble (1959) had reported better retention of the color of cabbage and broccoli cooked by boiling (in a large amount of water) than by microwave. The color of vegetables cooked by microwave was similar to that of vegetables cooked in a pressure saucepan.

Enzymes. Chlorophyll derivatives formed by the removal of the phytyl group by the enzyme chlorophyllase or by alkali are water soluble, which accounts for the greenish color sometimes seen in water that has been used for cooking green vegetables. Chlorophyllase activity results in formation of phytyl alcohol and chlorophyllide, a green, water-soluble derivative of chlorophyll. This enzyme occurs in many vegetables at varying levels. Spinach is rich in chlorophyllase, but the amount changes both with the season and with the variety (Weast and Mackinney, 1940). Some vegetables such as snap beans may not contain chlorophyllase (Jones et al., 1963). Chlorophyllase is more resistant to heat than many enzymes. It is quite active in water as hot as 66–75°C, but is destroyed by boiling (Clydesdale and Francis, 1968). Chlorophyllase also removes the phytyl group from pheophytin to form pheophorbide, which is similar in color to pheophytin. Pheophorbide may be formed during the brining of cucumbers (White et al., 1963) and the blanching of okra, cucumber, and turnip greens at 82°C (Jones et al., 1963). The enzyme is rapidly inactivated in those vegetables at 100°C and in spinach at 84.5°C (Resende et al., 1969).

Flavonoids

Flavonoid pigments and related compounds are widely distributed in plant tissue. These pigments are found in the vacuole of the cell dissolved in the cell sap. Flavonoids have a basic $C_6C_3C_6$ skeleton and consist of two benzene rings and a three-carbon chain that, together with oxygen, form a part of the central ring (Fig. 15.3). Hydroxyl (–OH), methoxyl (–OCH$_3$), or sugar groups are attached at various points on the skeleton. Most naturally occurring flavonoids are glycosides, meaning that a sugar moiety is present. The combinations of and locations of added groups influence the color of the pigment. Flavonoids include two major groups of related compounds, the anthocyanins and the anthoxanthins.

Anthocyanins

Color. Anthocyanins are red, purple, or blue pigments found in the cell sap of a number of fruits and in a few vegetables. Anthocyanins are responsible for the bright red skins of radishes, the red skins of potatoes, and the dark purple skin of eggplant. The color of red cabbage is due to the presence of an anthocyanin that is confined to layers of cells on the surface of the leaf. Fruits that contain anthocyanin pigments include blackberries, red and black raspberries, blueberries, cherries, currants, Concord and other red grapes, pomegranates, ripe gooseberries, and the red skin of apples. The

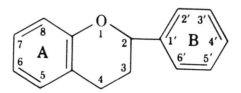

Figure 15.3. $C_6C_3C_6$ skeleton of flavonoid compounds. (From Paul, P. C. and Palmer, H. H. 1972. *Food Theory and Applications*, chapter 6, p. 283. Macmillan, New York. Reprinted with permission.)

color of anthocyanins varies with the molecular structure. As hydroxylation increases, blueness increases.

Structures. Anthocyanins contain hydroxyl groups at positions 3, 5, and 7 and are glycosides, in contrast to the corresponding sugar-free anthocyanidins, which are rare in nature. The sugar moiety usually is attached to the hydroxyl at position 3. Sugars found in the glycosides may be glucose, rhamnose, galactose, arabinose, fructose, and xylose. The sugar portion is responsible for the solubility. Substitutions on ring B result in formation of various anthocyanins as shown in Figure 15.4. Derivatives of cyanidin, such as the corresponding glycoside, cyanin, occur in apples, cherries, cranberries, currants, elderberries, purple figs, peaches, plums, raspberries, rhubarb, and purple turnips. Cyanidin has two hydroxyl groups attached to the phenyl ring in positions 3′ and 4′. Pelargonidin, a strawberry pigment, has a hydroxyl group at position 3′ and delphinidin, a pigment found in pomegranate, blueberries, and eggplant, has three hydroxyl groups that are located in the 3′, 4′, and 5′ positions. Other related anthocyanins have methoxyl groups in place of one or more of the hydroxyl groups of the molecule. The color of the anthocyanin varies with variations in molecular structures. As hydroxylation increases, blueness increases. Thus delphinidin is bluer than pelargonidin (Bate–Smith, 1954). As methylation of hydroxyl groups increases, redness increases (Shirkhande, 1976). Color of the anthocyanins also is influenced by the presence of other phenolic compounds. Other flavonoids form complexes with the glycosides of commonly occurring anthocyanins at pH levels ranging from 2 to 5. This

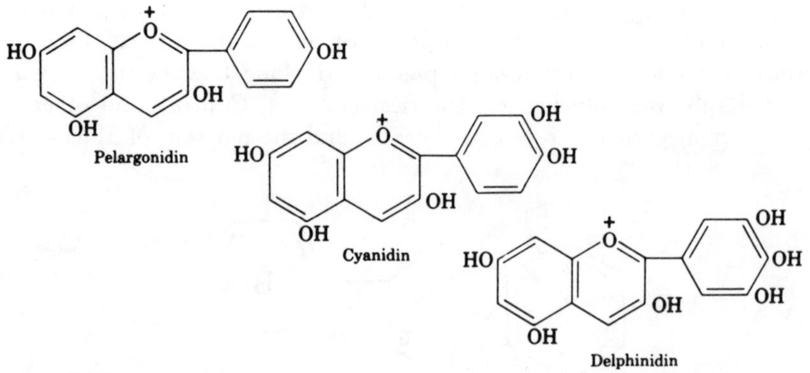

Figure 15.4. Pelargonidin, cyanidin, and delphinidin structures. (From Paul, P. C. and Palmer, H. H. 1972. *Food Theory and Applications*, chapter 6, p. 285. Macmillan, New York. Reprinted with permission.)

interaction increases the blueness of the anthocyanins (Asen et al., 1972). Carotenoids or chlorophyll may be found in tissue containing anthocyanins.

Stability—pH. Anthocyanins are electron-deficient. Therefore, they are very reactive and may undergo detrimental changes during processing and subsequent storage. Color varies with the pH. The molecule assumes the configuration of a cation in acid and is red in color. The color is most intense at very low pH values (Francis, 1975). Lowering the pH of anthocyanin solutions also decreases the lightness as measured by a color-difference meter (Van Buren et al., 1974). The molecule is uncharged at a neutral pH and is violet in color. In an alkaline medium, the anionic form exists and results in a blue color. The juice of some fruits and vegetables becomes greenish as alkali is added. This color probably is caused by the presence of flavones or flavonols with the anthocyanins. With the addition of alkali, the flavones or flavonols turn yellow, whereas the anthocyanins turn blue, and a mixture of the two colors appears green. Such a color change can be seen in red cabbage. The effects on the molecule of differences in hydrogen-ion concentration are illustrated with cyanidin, the most commonly occurring anthocyanidin (Robinson, 1942; Blank, 1947) (see Fig. 15.5).

Stability—metals. Anthocyanins that have two or more adjacent, un-substituted hydroxyl groups react with iron, aluminum, or tin to form greenish, blue, or slate-colored complexes. These metal chelates, the color of which depends on the metal involved and the chelation sites on the pigment, make the food unattractive. The effect of iron on the color of anthocyanin pigment can be demonstrated readily by shredding red cabbage with a nonstainless blade. Iron from the blade reacts with the pigment in the cabbage to form a dark blue complex. Acid will dissociate the iron-pigment chelate, as can be demonstrated by applying lemon juice to the discolored cabbage. The acid shifts the pigment to the red flavylium ion.

Because these pigments react with metals, foods that contain an-thocyanins are processed in enamel-lined tin cans instead of in unlined tin cans. Anthocyanin-containing foods may, however, cause pitting and perforation of the can. Small exposed areas of the two metals, such as at the seams or in imperfections in the enameled lining, together with the acidic fruit juice form an electrolytic cell that permits localized corrosion of the can. Anthocyanins contribute to the corrosion either by binding metal ions as they are dissolved by the acid or by removing hydrogen and so acting as a depolarizer (Cruess, 1958).

Stability—temperature. Although alteration in pH may bring about reversible changes in the color of anthocyanin pigments, profound and irreversible changes that result in deterioration of color may occur in the

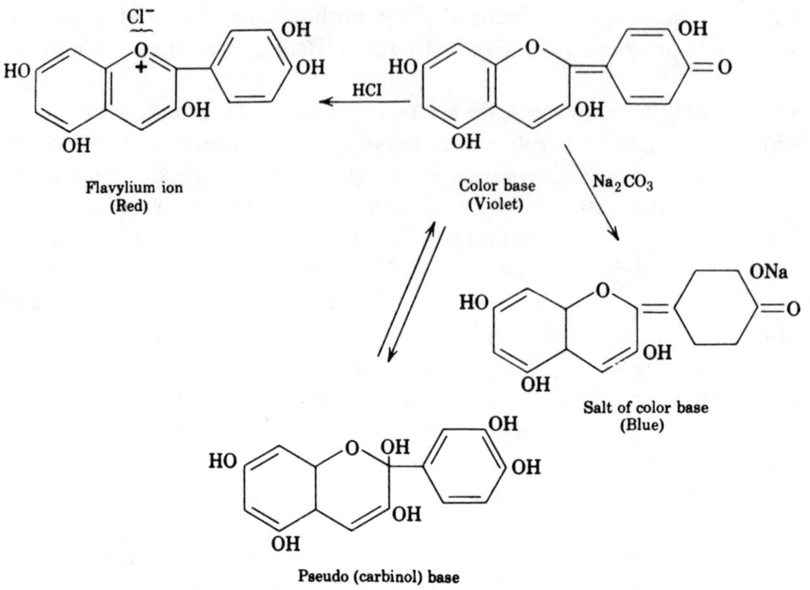

Figure 15.5. Flavylium ion, color base, salt of color base, and pseudo (carbinol) base structures (From Paul, P. C. and Palmer, H. H. 1972. *Food Theory and Applications*, chapter 6, p. 286. Macmillan, New York. Reprinted with permission.)

anthocyanin pigments in thermally processed fruit products. The pigment in strawberry preserves is markedly labile, a factor that limits the shelf life of the product or may make it unmarketable. Because of their acidity, most fruits containing anthocyanins usually do not suffer undesirable color changes in cooking. Red cabbage is the anthocyanin-containing vegetable most often cooked. When steamed or boiled in tap water, red cabbage turns a bluish color that many people consider unpleasant. The color can be changed to an attractive reddish color by the addition of acid during cooking. Loss of the bright-red color of the freshly made product is due not only to a decrease in the pelargonidin-3-monoglucoside but to development of a brownish degradation product as well (Meschter, 1953). A number of factors influence the rate at which the pigment decomposes and the color deteriorates. A high storage temperature, a high pH, oxygen in the head space, the presence of sugars, and the presence of ascorbic acid in the preserves all favor the destruction of anthocyanin pigment. Storage of the preserves at refrigerator temperature (4°C) increases the shelf life 6-fold over storage at room temperature and 60-fold over storage in a warm place (38°C). Aerobic oxidation of ascorbic acid in the preserves induces oxidation of the anthocyanin, leading to an undesirable brown color

(Sondheimer and Kertesz, 1953). These authors suggested that H_2O_2 arising from the oxidation of ascorbic acid to dehydroascorbic acid might be responsible for the oxidation of the pigment. A low pH favors retention of color (Meschter, 1953; Lukton et al., 1956), presumably by keeping the pigment shifted from the unstable pseudobase to the more stable flavylium form (Sondheimer, 1953). A low pH is particularly advantageous when oxygen is present in the headspace (Lukton et al., 1956). Sugars, especially fructose, accelerate the destruction of the pigment. Degradation products of sugar are thought to be responsible, and both furfural and hydroxyfurfural have been shown to promote degradation (Meschter, 1953; Tinsley and Bockian, 1960).

Stability—enzymes. Hydrolysis of the 3-glycosidic group may be caused by an enzyme (see Fig. 15.6). The anthocyanidin is unstable to oxidative degradation. Phenolases may be indirectly involved through enzymatic oxidation of catechol to a quinone that oxidizes the anthocyanin. The involvement of enzymes has not been described completely (Jurd, 1972). The products of ascorbic acid oxidation, as well as sulfur dioxide, and furfural and hydroxymethyl-furfural, products of sugar degradation, exert a detrimental effect on the anthocyanins (Shirkhande, 1976).

Anthoxanthins

Color. The pigments of this group are almost colorless or pale yellow. Like the anthocyanins, they are water soluble and occur in the vacuoles of plant cells. They may occur alone in light-colored vegetables such as potatoes and yellow-skinned onions, or with other pigments such as anthocyanins. They are so widely distributed that it is exceptional to find a plant in which anthoxanthins are not present. They frequently occur in complex mixtures.

Structures. Anthoxanthin is a term given to a group of compounds including flavones, flavonols, and flavonones. Skeletal structures for the

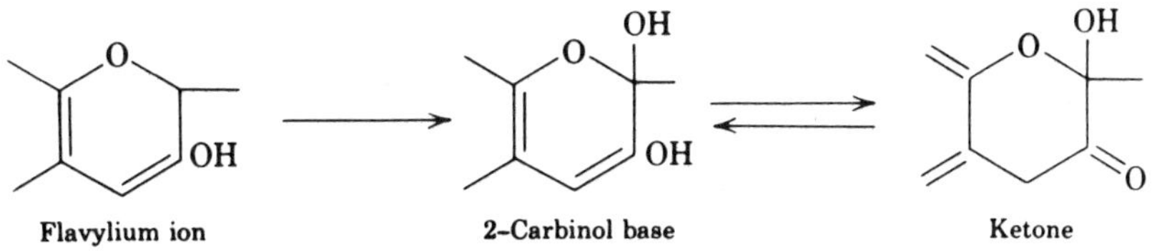

Flavylium ion   2-Carbinol base   Ketone

Figure 15.6. Flavylium ion, 2-carbinol base, and ketone structures. (From Paul, P. C. and Palmer, H. H. 1972. *Food Theory and Applications*, chapter 6, p. 288. Macmillan, New York. Reprinted with permission.)

three are shown in Figure 15.7. The sugar moiety of the glycosidic form usually is attached on the A ring at position 7, as shown in Figure 15.7.

Stability—pH. The anthoxanthins turn yellow in the presence of alkali. The color of white vegetables often can be improved by adding an acidic compound such as cream of tartar to the cooking water, but at the expense of some firming of the tissues.

Stability—metals. Anthoxanthins also have the ability to chelate metals, which also may result in discoloration. Iron salts cause a brownish discoloration. Traces of iron salts in alkaline tap water may react with anthoxanthins and other closely related phenolic compounds to produce

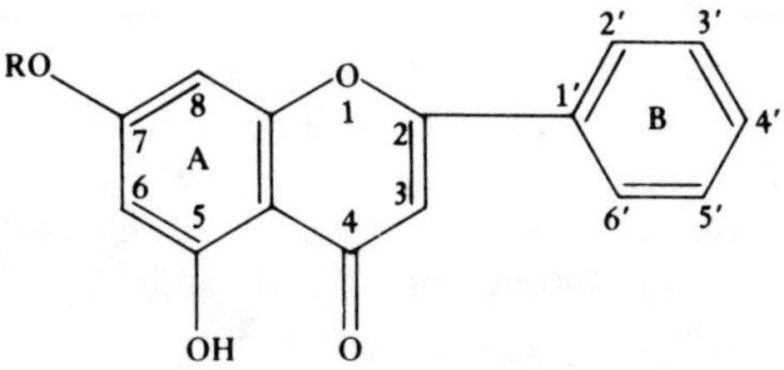

Flavone

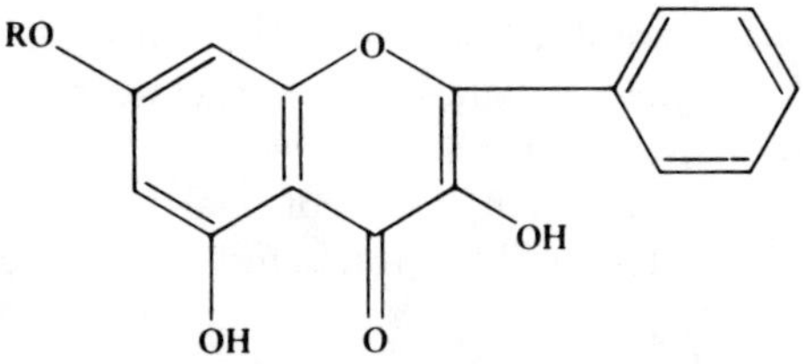

Flavonol

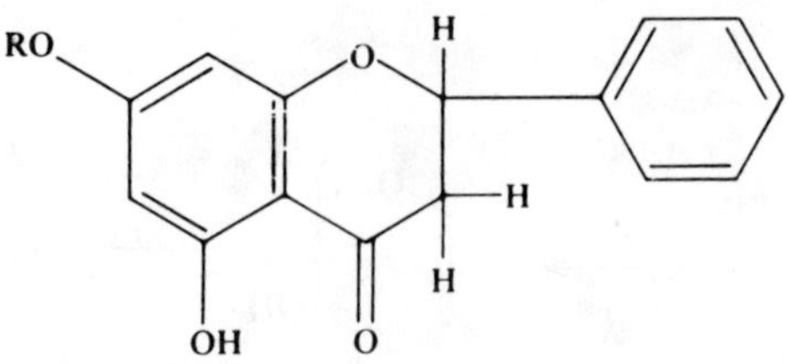

Flavonone

Figure 15.7. Structures of flavone, flavonol, and flavonone. (From Campbell, A. M., Penfield, M. P., and Griswold, R. M. 1979. *The Experimental Study of Food*, chapter 6, p. 183. Houghton Mifflin, Boston. Reprinted with permission.)

some of the yellow-to-brown discoloration often seen in cooked white vegetables. Yellow-skinned onions cooked in alkaline water are especially likely to show such a change. Similar results are seen if an aluminum pan is used.

Blackening of potatoes after cooking is attributed to formation of a dark-colored complex between iron and chlorogenic acid in potatoes with low organic acid content. Organic acids such as citric acid chelate metals so that they are not available to react with chlorogenic acid (Heisler et al., 1964). Cauliflower may become discolored because flavonol glycosides complex with ferrous or stannous ions. Thus lacquered cans are used for cauliflower (Chandler, 1964). Asparagus contains a flavonol, rutin, which precipitates as yellow crystals from the liquid of asparagus canned in glass containers. This precipitate is not found in asparagus canned in tin containers because rutin forms a light yellow complex with stannous ions. The complex is more soluble than rutin so precipitation does not occur (Dame et al., 1959). Sweet potatoes form yellow complexes with tin and dark greenish complexes with iron. Use of tin cans rather than enamel-lined cans with sweet potatoes provides tin to compete with the iron for complex formation and prevents darkening (Scott et al., 1974; Twigg et al., 1974).

Leucoanthocyanins
Another group of flavonoid compounds important to the color of some canned foods is composed of leucoanthocyanins, colorless phenolic compounds sometimes referred to as proanthocyanins. These compounds are converted to anthocyanin when subjected to boiling hydrochloric acid. Some products may become pink or red as a result of this conversion. The pink color that sometimes develops in canned pears has been identified as tin--cyanidin complex. The compound forming the complex with tin is formed by the oxidation of leucoanthocyanins (Chandler and Clegg, 1970). Leucoanthocyanins also may be responsible for the pinking of sauerkraut (Gorin and Jans, 1971) and applesauce (Singleton, 1972).

OBJECTIVES

1. To be able to identify the major plant-pigment categories and food products associated with the classifications.
2. To observe the effects of pH and temperature on plant pigments.
3. To observe the effects of metals and temperature on plant pigments.
4. To explain the conversion of chlorophyll pigments to pheophytins and the factors effecting this reaction.
5. To determine the water or lipid solubility of plant pigments.
6. To be able to define chlorophylls, carotenoids, anthocyanins and anthoxanthins, plant-cell sap, chlorophyllase, pheophytin, and flavonoids.

7. To discuss the factors influencing plant-pigment stability and/or degradation.

MATERIALS

spinach, frozen, chopped	$1/2$ lb
broccoli, frozen, chopped	$1/2$ lb
green snap beans, frozen	$1/2$ lb
red cabbage, fresh	$1/2$ lb
blueberries, frozen	$1/2$ lb
carrots, fresh	$1/2$ lb
sweet potatoes or yams, fresh	$1/2$ lb
cauliflower, frozen	$1/2$ lb
white potatoes, fresh	$1/2$ lb
pipet fillers	5
test tubes, disposable glass culture (19 ml capacity)	100
test tube racks	8
eye droppers	18
blenders	18
buffer standards (pH 3, 5, 7, 9)	150 ml each
saucepans, 1 qt	18
beakers, 250 ml	18
beakers, 150 ml	18
funnels, glass	18
filter paper, #1 or #4, general purpose (12.5 cm)	25 sheets
pH meters	2
volumetric flasks, 50 ml	4
pipets (10 ml) or graduated cylinders	36
ferric chloride ($FeCl_3$), anhydrous	0.3 g
cupric sulfate ($CuSO_4$), anhydrous	0.4 g
magnesium sulfate ($MgSO_4$), anhydrous	0.3 g
stannous chloride ($SnCl_2$), anhydrous	0.5 g
acetone	1 L
water, distilled	1 L
masking tape	1 roll

REAGENT PREPARATION

The laboratory instructors will prepare the following salt solutions before the pigment laboratory session.

$FeCl_3$	0.1 N	
$CuSO_4$	0.1 N	
$MgSO_4$	0.1 N	
$SnCl_2$	0.1 N	

FeCl$_3$. To make up 0.1 N FeCl$_3$, place 0.27 g FeCl$_3$ into a 50 ml volumetric flask. Bring up to volume with distilled H$_2$O. Shake until dissolved. Label the volumetric flask.

CuSO$_4$. To make up 0.1 N CuSO$_4$, place 0.4 g CuSO$_4$ into a 50 ml volumetric flask. Bring up to volume with distilled H$_2$O. Shake until dissolved. Label the volumetric flask.

MgSO$_4$. To make up 0.1 N MgSO$_4$, place 0.3 g MgSO$_4$ into a 50 ml volumetric flask. Bring up to volume with distilled H$_2$O. Shake until dissolved. Label the volumetric flask.

SnCl$_2$. To make up 0.1 N SnCl$_4$, place 0.47 g SnCl$_2$ into a 50 ml volumetric flask. Bring up to volume with distilled H$_2$O. Shake until dissolved. Label the volumetric flask.

PIGMENT EXTRACTION—
FORMULATION AND EXTRACTION PROCEDURES

Spinach/Broccoli/Green Beans/Carrots/Sweet Potatoes

vegetable	100 g
acetone	80 ml
water, distilled	20 ml

Pigment Extraction

1. Weigh or measure all of the ingredients using top-loading balances and/or graduated cylinders.
2. Place 100 g of vegetable into a blender containing 80 ml acetone plus 20 ml water. Blend for 2 min.
3. Place a piece of filter paper onto a glass funnel. Filter the vegetable slurry into a 150 ml beaker. Save the filtrate. This contains the pigment to be used for the experiment. Discard the vegetable residue.

Red Cabbage/Blueberries/Cauliflower/White Potatoes

fruit or vegetable	100 g
water, distilled	100 ml

Pigment Extraction

1. Weigh or measure all of the ingredients using top-loading balances and/or graduated cylinders.
2. Place 100 g of vegetable or fruit into a blender containing 100 ml distilled water. Blend for 2 min.

3. Place a piece of filter paper onto a glass funnel. Filter the slurry into a 150 ml beaker. Save the filtrate. This contains the pigment to be used for the experiment. Discard the vegetable or fruit residue.

PROCEDURES—EFFECT OF pH AND TEMPERATURE ON PLANT PIGMENTS

1. Label four test tubes pH 3, pH 5, pH 7, pH 9 (one test tube per solution).
2. Place 10 ml of either pH 3, 5, 7, or 9 buffered solutions into the appropriately marked test tube.
3. With an eye dropper, drop the fruit or vegetable filtrate into the test tube containing the pH 3 buffered solution. Swirl the test tube after each drop. Count the number of drops required to change the color of the solution. Record the number of drops plus original filtrate color and color change on the plant pigment pH and temperature effects data sheet.
4. Put this same number of drops of filtrate into each of the other test tubes. Swirl this mixture. Observe the color and record these data on the plant pigment pH and temperature effects data sheet.
5. Next, place the four tubes into a 250 ml beaker containing water and place this container into a boiling water bath (1 qt saucepan) for 10 min. Note and record the color in the four test tubes after heat treatment on the plant pigment pH and temperature effects data sheet.
6. Display the tubes for class evaluation.

VARIABLES

1. Effects of pH and temperature on plant pigments (for all variables follow the procedures for investigating the effects of pH and temperature on plant pigments)
   (a) *Spinach*. Conduct the pigment extraction procedure for spinach. Use the spinach filtrate.
   (b) *Broccoli*. Conduct the pigment extraction procedure for broccoli. Use the broccoli filtrate.
   (c) *Green beans*. Conduct the pigment extraction procedure for green beans. Use the green bean filtrate.
   (d) *Carrots*. Conduct the pigment extraction procedure for carrots. Use the carrot filtrate.
   (e) *Sweet potatoes*. Conduct the pigment extraction procedure for sweet potatoes. Use the sweet potato filtrate.
   (f) *Red cabbage*. Conduct the pigment extraction procedure for red cabbage. Use the red cabbage filtrate.
   (g) *Blueberries*. Conduct the pigment extraction procedure for blueberries. Use the blueberry filtrate.

(h) *Cauliflower.* Conduct the pigment extraction procedure for cauliflower. Use the cauliflower filtrate.

(i) *White potatoes.* Conduct the pigment extraction procedure for white potatoes. Use the white potato filtrate.

PROCEDURES—EFFECT OF METALS AND TEMPERATURE ON PLANT PIGMENTS

1. Label four test tubes $FeCl_3$, $CuSO_4$, $MgSO_4$, $SnCl_2$ (one test tube per solution).
2. Place 2 ml of either $FeCl_3$, $CuSO_4$, $MgSO_4$, or $SnCl_2$ into the appropriately marked test tube.
3. Add 10 ml of the fruit or vegetable filtrate to each of the four test tubes. Swirl the test tube. Record the original filtrate color and the color change on the plant pigment metals and temperature effects data sheet.
4. Next, place the four tubes into a 250 ml beaker containing water and place this container into a boiling-water bath (1 qt saucepan) for 10 min. Note and record the color in the four test tubes after heat treatment on the plant pigment metals and temperature effects data sheet.
5. Display the tubes for class evaluation.

VARIABLES

1. Effect of metals and temperature on plant pigments (for all variables follow the procedures for investigating the effects of metals and temperature on plant pigments)

   (a) *Spinach.* Conduct the pigment extraction procedure for spinach. Use the spinach filtrate.

   (b) *Broccoli.* Conduct the pigment extraction procedure for broccoli. Use the broccoli filtrate.

   (c) *Green beans.* Conduct the pigment extraction procedure for green beans. Use the green bean filtrate.

   (d) *Carrots.* Conduct the pigment extraction procedure for carrots. Use the carrot filtrate.

   (e) *Sweet potatoes.* Conduct the pigment extraction procedure for sweet potatoes. Use the sweet potato filtrate.

   (f) *Red cabbage.* Conduct the pigment extraction procedure for red cabbage. Use the red cabbage filtrate.

   (g) *Blueberries.* Conduct the pigment extraction procedure for blueberries. Use the blueberry filtrate.

   (h) *Cauliflower.* Conduct the pigment extraction procedure for cauliflower. Use the cauliflower filtrate.

(i) **White potatoes**. Conduct the pigment extraction procedure for white potatoes. Use the white potato filtrate.

ASSESSMENT

Subjective Measurements

Visual
Note the colors of the solutions for each of the plant pigments at each pH and metal being tested; notations should be made before and after heating the test tubes in the water bath. Record the data on the plant pigment data sheets.

STUDY QUESTIONS

1. Cite the three major plant pigment categories and their major subdivisions along with food products associated with the classifications.
2. Compare the colors of the following pigments at a pH range of 3–9: chlorophylls, carotenoids, anthocyanins, anthoxanthins.
   (a) Within each pigment category are there color changes over a pH range of 3–9? Why or why not?
   (b) Within each pigment category, are there differences between unheated versus heated pigments over a pH range of 3–9? Why or why not?
   (c) Do various pigment categories respond to pH changes differently?
3. Compare the colors of the following pigments in the metal salt solutions of $FeCl_3$, $CuSO_4$, $MgSO_4$, and $SnCl_2$: chlorophylls, carotenoids, anthocyanins, anthoxanthins.
   (a) Within each pigment category are there color changes using different salts? Why or why not?
   (b) Within each pigment category, are there differences between unheated versus heated pigments using different salts? Why or why not?
   (c) Do various pigment categories respond to metals differently?
4. When heating chlorophyll-containing vegetables such as green beans, why does the color change from a bright green to a dull olive brown?
   (a) Why does this occur more readily in a closed container as compared to heating in an open container?
   (b) How can this discoloration be minimized?
   (c) Would we see color differences if the beans were heated in distilled water versus tap water? Why or why not?
5. Does the pH of the cooking liquid change as fruits or vegetables are heated? Why or why not?

6. Plant pigments differ in their solubility characteristics. Cite whether the major plant pigments are lipid or water soluble.
7. Define chlorophylls, carotenoids, anthocyanins, anthoxanthins, plant-cell sap, chlorophyllase, pheophytin, flavonoid.
8. How does blanching influence plant pigmentation?
9. Discuss the factors influencing plant pigment stability and/or degradation.
10. When heating a red cabbage, apples are sometimes added to the cooking medium. What effect does the addition of apples have on the plant pigment? Why?

SELECTED BIBLIOGRAPHY

Asen, S., Stewart, R. N., and Norris, K. H. 1972. Co-pigmentation of anthocyanins in plant tissues and its effect on color. *Phytochemistry* **11**:1139.

Bate-Smith, E. C. 1954. Flavonoid compounds in foods. *Adv. Food Res.* **5**:261.

Blank, F. 1947. The anthocyanin pigments of plants. *Botan. Rev.* **13**:241.

Borchgrevink, N. C. and Charley, H. 1966. Color of cooked carrots related to carotene content. *J. Am. Dietet. Assoc.* **49**:116.

Campbell, A. M., Penfield, M. P., and Griswold, R. M. 1979. *The Experimental Study of Food*, chapter 6. Houghton Mifflin Co., Boston.

Chandler, B. V. 1964. Discoloration of processed cauliflower. *Food Preserv. Q.* **24**:11.

Chandler, B. V. and Clegg, K. M. 1970. Pink discoloration in canned pears. I. Role of tin in pigment formation. *J. Sci. Food Agric.* **21**:315.

Chapman, V. J., Putz, J. O., Gilpin, G. L., Sweeney, J. P., and Eisen, J. N. 1960. Electronic cooking of fresh and frozen broccoli. *J. Home Econ.* **52**:161.

Charley, H. 1982. *Food Science*, chapters 27, 28. John Wiley & Sons, New York.

Clydesdale, F. M., Fleishman, D. L., and Francis, F. J. 1970. Maintenance of color in processed green vegetables. *Food Prod. Dev.* **4**(5):127.

Clydesdale, F. M. and Francis, F. J. 1968. Chlorophyll changes in thermally processed spinach as influenced by enzyme conversion and pH adjustment. *Food Technol.* **22**:793.

Cruess, W. V. 1958. Corrosion and perforation in tin plate. In *Commercial Fruit and Vegetable Products*, p. 305. McGraw-Hill, New York.

Dame, C., Chichester, C. O., and Marsh, G. L. 1959. Studies of processed all-green asparagus. IV. Studies on the influence of tin on the solubility of rutin and on the concentration of rutin present in the brines of asparagus processed in glass and tin containers. *Food Res.* **24**:28.

Della Monica, E. S. and McDowell, P. E. 1965. Comparison of beta-carotene content of dried carrots prepared by three dehydration processes. *Food Technol.* **19**:1597.

Dutton, H. J., Bailey, G. F., and Kohake, E. 1943. Dehydrated spinach. Changes in color and pigments during processing and storage. *Ind. Eng. Chem.* **35**:1173.

Eheart, M. S. and Gott, C. 1965. Chlorophyll, ascorbic acid, and pH changes in green vegetables cooked by stir fry, microwave, and conventional methods and a comparison of chlorophyll methods. *Food Technol.* **19**:867.

Francis, F. J. 1975. Anthocyanins as food colors. *Food Technol.* **29**(5):52.

Fuleki, T. 1969. Anthocyanins of strawberry, rhubarb, radish, and onion. *J. Food Sci.* **34**:365.

Gold, H. J. and Weckel, K. G. 1959. Degradation of chlorophyll to pheophytin during sterilization of canned green peas by heat. *Food Technol.* **13**:281.

Gordon, J. and Noble, I. 1959. Effect of cooking method on vegetables. *J. Am. Dietet. Assoc.* **35**:578.

Gorin, N. and Jans, J. A. 1971. Discoloration of sauerkraut probably caused by a leucoanthocyanidin. *J. Food Sci.* **36**:943.

Heisler, E. G., Siciliano, J., Woodward, C. F., and Porter, W. L. 1964. After cooking discoloration of potatoes. Role of the organic acids. *J. Food Sci.* **29**:555.

Jones, I. D., White, R. C., and Gibbs, E. 1963. Influence of blanching and brining treatments on the formation of chlorophyllides, pheophytins, and pheophorbides in green plant tissue. *J. Food Sci.* **28**:437.

Jurd, L. 1972. Some advances in the chemistry of anthocyanin-type plant pigments. In *The Chemistry of Plant Pigments*, Chichester, C. O. (Ed.). Academic Press, New York.

Labuza, T. P. 1973. Effects of processing, storage, and handling on nutrient retention in foods. Effects of dehydration and storage. *Food Technol.* **27**(1):20.

Lukton, A., Chichester, C. O., and Mackinney, G. 1956. The breakdown of strawberry anthocyanin pigment. *Food Technol.* **10**:427.

Mackinney, G. and Joslyn, M. A. 1940. The conversion of chlorophyll to pheophytin. *J. Am. Chem. Soc.* **32**:392.

Mackinney, G. and Weast, C. A. 1940. Color changes in green vegetables. *Ind. Eng. Chem.* **32**:392.

Markakis, P., Jarczyk, A., and Khrishna, S. P. 1963. Nonvolatile acids in blueberries. *J. Agric. Food Chem.* **11**:8.

Meschter, E. E. 1953. Effect of carbohydrates and other factors on strawberry products. *J. Agric. Food Chem.* **1**:574.

Meyer, L. H. 1982. *Food Chemistry*, chapter 7. AVI Publishing, Westport, CT.

Noble, A. C. 1975. Investigation of the color changes in heat-concentrated tomato pulp. *J. Agric. Food Chem.* **23**:48.

Paul, P. C. and Palmer, H. H. 1972. *Food Theory and Applications*, chapter 6. John Wiley & Sons, New York.

Purcell, A. E., Walter, W. M. Jr., and Thompkins, W. T. 1969. Relationship of vegetable color to physical state of the carotenes. *J. Agric. Food Chem.* **17**:41.

Resende, R., Francis, F. J., and Stumbo, C. R. 1969. Thermal destruction and regeneration of enzymes in green beans and spinach puree. *Food Technol.* **23**:63.

Robinson, R. 1942. The red and blue coloring matter of plants. *Endeavour* **1**:92.

Schwartz, J. H., Greenspun, R. B., and Porter, W. L. 1962. Identification and determination of the major acids of the white potato. *J. Agric. Food Chem.* **10**:43.

Scott, L. E., Twigg, B. A., and Bouwkamp, J. C. 1974. Color of processed sweet potatoes: Effects of can type. *J. Food Sci.* **39**:563.

Shirkande, A. J. 1976. Anthocyanins in foods. *CRC Critical Reviews in Food Sci. Nutr.* **7**:193.

Singleton, V. L. 1972. Common plant phenols other than anthocyanins, contributions to coloration and discoloration. In *The Chemistry of Plant Pigments*, Chichester, C. O. (Ed.). Academic Press, New York.

Sistrunk, W. A. and Cash, J. N. 1970. The effect of certain chemicals on the color and polysaccharides of strawberry puree. *Food Technol.* **24**:473.

Skalski, C. and Sistrunk, W. A. 1973. Factors influencing color degradation in Concord grape juice. *J. Food Sci.* **38**:1060.

Sondheimer, E. 1953. On the relation between spectral changes and pH of the anthocyanin pelargonidin-3-monoglucoside. *J. Am. Chem. Soc.* **75**:1507.

Sondheimer, E. and Kertesz, A. I. 1953. Participation of ascorbic acid in the destruction of anthocyanin in strawberry juice and model systems. *Food Res.* **18**:475.

Stephens, T. S. and McLemore, T. A. 1969. Preparation and storage of dehydrated carrot flakes. *Food Technol.* **23**:1600.

Sweeney, J. P. 1970. Improved chlorophyll retention in green beans held on a steam table. *Food Technol.* **24**:490.

Sweeney, J. P. and Martin, M. 1958. Determination of chlorophyll and pheophytin in broccoli heated by various procedures. *Food Res.* **23**:635.

Sweeney, J. P. and Martin, M. E. 1961. Stability of chlorophyll in vegetables as affected by pH. *Food Technol.* **15**:263.

Tinsley, I. J. and Bockian, A. H. 1960. Some effects of sugars on the breakdown of pelargonidin-3-glucoside in model systems at 90° C. *Food Res.* **25**:161.

Twigg, B. A., Scott, L. E., and Bouwkamp, J. C. 1974. Color of processed sweet potatoes: Effect of additives. *J. Food Sci.* **39**:565.

VanBuren, J. P., Hrazdina, G., and Robinson, W. B. 1974. Color of anthocyanin solutions expressed in lightness and chromaticity terms. Effect of pH and type of anthocyanin. *J. Food Sci.* **39**:325.

VanBuren, J. P., Moyer, J. C., and Robinson, W. B. 1964. Chlorophyll losses in blanched snap beans. *Food Technol.* **18**:1204.

Walker, G. C. 1964. Color determination in frozen French beans (*Phaseolus vulgaris*). II. The effect of blanching. *J. Food Sci.* **29**:389.

Weast, C. A. and Mackinney, G. 1940. Chlorophyllase. *J. Biol. Chem.* **133**:551.

White, R. C., Jones, I. D., and Gibbs., E. 1963. Determination of chlorophylls, chlorophyllides, pheophytins, and pheophorbides in plant materials. *J. Food Sci.* **28**:431.

Williams, M. and Hrazdina, G. 1979. Anthocyanins as food colorants: Effects of pH on the formation of anthocyanin–rutin complexes. *J. Food Sci.* **44**:66.

Willstätter, R. and Stoll, A. 1928. *Investigations on Chlorophyll.* The Science Press Printing Co., Lancaster, PA.

Wrolstad, R. E. and Erlandson, J. A. 1973. Effect of metal ions on the color of strawberry puree. *J. Food Sci.* **38**:460.

Wrolstad, R. E., Putnam, T. P., and Varseveld, G. W. 1970. Color quality of frozen strawberries: Effect of anthocyanin, pH, total acidity, and ascorbic acid variability. *J. Food Sci.* **25**:448.

DATA SHEET
PLANT PIGMENTS: PH AND TEMPERATURE EFFECTS

NAME _____

DATE _____

VARIABLES	ORIGINAL COLOR	NO. OF DROPS	pH (UNHEATED)				pH (HEATED)			
			3	5	7	9	3	5	7	9
pH and T⁰ Spinach										
Broccoli										
Green beans										
Carrots										
Sweet potatoes										
Red cabbage										
Blueberries										
Cauliflower										
White potatoes										

DATA SHEET
PLANT PIGMENTS: METALS AND TEMPERATURE EFFECTS

NAME _____
DATE _____

VARIABLES	ORIGINAL COLOR	UNHEATED				HEATED			
		$FeCl_3$	$CuSO_4$	$MgSO_4$	$SnCl_2$	$FeCl_3$	$CuSO_4$	$MgSO_4$	$SnCl_2$
Metals and T⁰ Spinach									
Broccoli									
Green beans									
Carrots									
Sweet potatoes									
Red cabbage									
Blueberries									
Cauliflower									
White potatoes									

Appendix A

Equipment Instructions

METTLER TOP-LOADING BALANCE WEIGHING INSTRUCTIONS

General View (Fig. A.1)

1.	Overlap adjustment	8.	Optical scale
2.	Leveling	9.	Focus adjustment screw
3.	Level indicator	10.	Image brightness adjustment
4.	Zero adjustment knob	11.	Light switch
5.	Tare indicator	12.	Tare knob
6.	Digital readout knob	13.	Weighing pan
7.	Filling guide		

Directions for Use (Fig. A.2)

- Switch on power
- Set tare to zero by turning knob 12 in direction of arrow until stop position is reached.
- E200, E2000: Bring digital readout to "00" by turning knob 6.
- Adjust zero point.

Weight Determination

- Place sample on pan.
- E1000: Read result (estimate tenths of grams by the position of the pointer between scale divisions).
- E200, E2000: Turn knob 6 until the next lower scale division line is exactly in the center of the illuminated gap of the index fork.
- Read result.

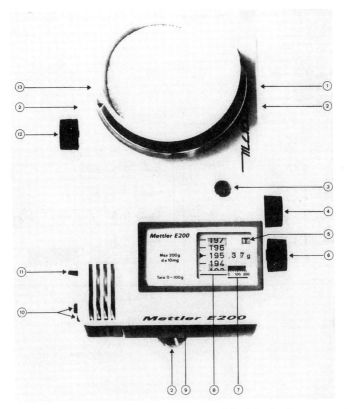

Figure A.1. General view of balance. (Courtesy of the Mettler Instrument Corp., Hightstown, NJ.)

ELECTRONIC BALANCES INSTRUCTIONS

Keyboard Functions (Fig. A.3)

There are only three keys for all SERIES 7000A balances, which are simple to operate. The keys are membrane switches that require only light pressure to activate.

1. AutoCal key is for calibration purposes only. See AUTOCAL for complete description. Students do not use!!!
2. Tare key is for taring/zeroing of the unit. See TARING section.
3. Function key is for changing modes. SERIES 7000A balances will weigh in four separate modes: grams, av. oz, pennyweight, and/or grains/pounds. Simply press the Function key until the appropriate mode indicator appears at the left of the LED viewing window.

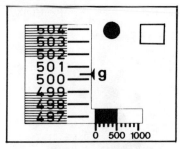

E1000: 500,4 g

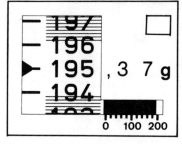

E200: 195,37 g

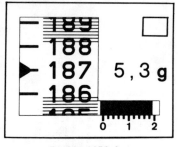

E2000: 1875,3 g

Figure A.2. Weight determination. (Courtesy of the Mettler Instrument Corp., Hightstown, NJ.)

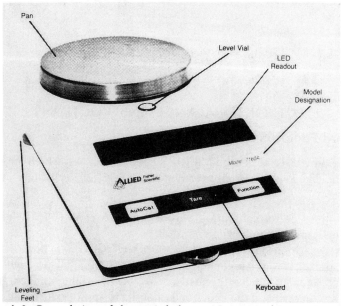

Figure A.3. General view of electronic balance. (Courtesy of Denver Instruments, Detroit, MI.)

Taring/Zeroing

To Tare or Zero the balance, simply press the Tare key; an audible beep and all "0's" on the display will indicate the container weight has been subtracted. A quick depression of the key may not tare the balance.

The SERIES 7000A have tare capabilities up to their total capacity, for obtaining actual weight of more than one sample at a time on the weighing pan. Place sample container on the weighing pan. Tare balance to "0." Place sample to be weighed in the container and read the results—the LED will show only the weight of the sample placed in the container. Continuous taring may be done and additional samples weighed until the total capacity of the balance has been exceeded. When the capacity is exceeded the LED will show "EEEEEEE."

VOLUME BY SEED DISPLACEMENT INSTRUCTIONS

Volume by seed displacement is determined by subtracting the volume of rapeseed required to fill the empty container from the measured volume of rapeseed required to fill a given container that holds the object for which volume is being measured. Rapeseeds are used because they are very lightweight and will not crush the baked product.

TO PREPARE THE PRODUCT, COVER WITH A SINGLE LAYER OF FOOD WRAP (avoid bulky overlaps as these add volume!).

The National Loaf Volumeter is often used for this determination (Fig. A.4).

A.	Latches on Upper Chamber	E.	Lower Chamber
B.	Upper Chamber	F.	Plate
C.	Lever	G.	Pivot
D.	Latch on Lower Chamber	H.	Scale

Directions for Use

1. Place the volumeter firmly on the laboratory bench.
2. To fill with rapeseeds, release the latches on the upper chamber and put the seeds into Chamber B. Lever C should be closed (in). Replace lid and tightly secure both top latches (A).
3. Making sure latch D is closed, open latch C and allow rapeseeds to free fall into chamber E. Read volume of empty chamber in cubic centimeters on scale H.
4. Return seeds to upper chamber A by holding plate F firmly to the edge of the table and inverting the volumeter 180° using pivot G. Lever C should be open (out) until all the seeds have fallen. NOW CLOSE LEVER C.

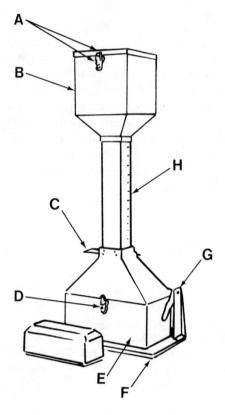

Figure A.4. National loaf volumeter.

5. Open latch D and place the baked product in the lower chamber. Close latch D securely.
6. Repeat step 3 and record the volume of the container and object in cubic centimeters.
7. Repeat step 4 to remove seeds. Be sure lever C is closed after seeds are in the upper chamber.
8. Carefully open latch D and remove the baked product. Seeds may adhere to the film so brush back into lower box E.
9. CALCULATION:

Volume of box E + product (cc) – volume of box E empty (cc) = volume of product (cc).

NOTE: The same principle can be used with any type of container that can be filled and leveled. Because the seeds tend to scatter, always have a second larger container underneath to collect spills. The volume of seeds can be measured in any appropriate graduated cylinder.

BAILEY SHORTOMETER INSTRUCTIONS

Key to Figure A.5

1. "On–off" switch
2. Button to push to lower pressure beam
3. Button to push to raise pressure beam
4. Reading dial (units are in ounces)
5. Insert sample

Directions for Use

1. Raise beam by pumping button #3.
2. Insert sample of uniform thickness in area #5.
3. Turn on current (switch #1).
4. Push in button #2 and continue pushing button until blade on beam cuts completely through sample.
5. Record pressure required to break sample (#4).
6. Turn current off (switch #1).

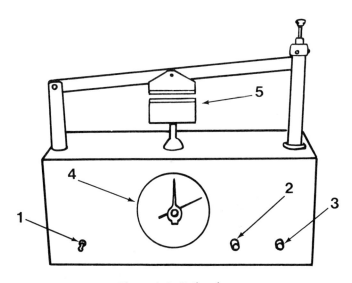

Figure A.5. Bailey shortometer.

WARNER-BRATZLER SHEAR INSTRUCTIONS

A.	Square	D.	Triangle
B.	Column	E.	Switch
C.	Dial	F.	Plate

This instrument (Fig. A.6) was developed to determine the pounds of force necessary to shear a core of meat but has also been used to determine the shear of other products.

Preparation of Sample

Using a twisting motion, cut a core of meat $1/2$ or 1 in. in diameter so that the cutting is parallel with the muscle fibers. All samples in one study should use the same size core. Carefully remove the meat from the core. You may need to use a rod (or pencil) to push the product out. Immediately wrap the product in food wrap to prevent surface drying.

Directions for Use

1. Plug instrument in.
2. Make sure column B is all the way up and square A is pushed in.
3. Make sure dial C is at 0.

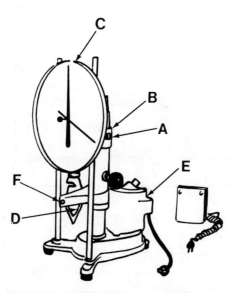

Figure A.6. Warner–Bratzler shear apparatus. (Courtesy of G.R. Electric Manufacturing Company, Manhattan, KS.)

4. Unwrap meat, and place meat cylinder in triangle D so that about $3/4$ in. is through the triangle. Loosely support both ends so that cylinder is level.
5. Turn on switch E.
6. Watch the dial for the maximum shear reading (pointer hand should stay at maximum reading but it sometimes jumps—reading hands will go back to 0). Record pounds of force/diameter of shear used.
7. Leave the machine on until the down stroke is complete. Turn the switch off.
8. Raise B to the full upright position and push A in.
9. Repeat to take a total of three readings that are cored at least $3/4$ in. apart from the meat tissue.
10. Report the average of three shear determinations.
11. After finishing, unplug, remove plates F and metal piece D. Wash and replace.

CARVER PRESS INSTRUCTIONS

The Carver Press (Fig. A.7) is a hydraulic system that is used in food research to press extractable juices from meat. These juices are primarily unbound water but also contain lipid substances.

Preparation of Sample

1. Cut the meat sample into $1/4$ in. cubes and weigh a 2.0–2.5 g sample to 0.01 g. For ground meat, use 1.5–2.0 g.
2. Place the meat at the center of a 3 in. canvas pad and cover with a second canvas pad.
3. Place this assembly first between two felt pads and then between metal discs.

NOTE: Two or three assemblies can be pressed at once (label each). Follow the same procedure but only one set of metal discs is used.

Directions for Use

1. Raise the heavy metal cylinder and place on support B.
2. Place the sample assembly centered on the platform so the metal cylinder will fit over the sample assembly.
3. Lower the metal cylinder A as shown in the figure. NEVER APPLY PRESSURE WITH THE CYLINDER RESTING ON B!
4. Close the release valve C.
5. Using handle D, pump the press until it becomes difficult.

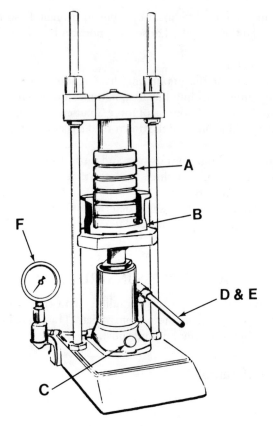

Figure A.7. Carver press. (Courtesy of Fred S. Carver, Inc., Menomonee, WI.)

6. Place the long handle E over handle D and continue pumping until gauge F reads 15,000 psi. You will need to pump slightly to keep 15,000 psi during the holding period. Hold for 3 min.
7. Release the pressure by opening valve C.
8. Push up cylinder (A) and rest on B.
9. Remove the samples, scrape the meat from the canvas pads and reweigh the sample.
10. Wash the canvas and felt pads in hot soapy bleach water, rinse, and place on the cake racks to dry. Wash the cylinder and the platform of press.
11. CALCULATION

$$\% \text{ press fluid} = \frac{\text{original wt. (g)} - \text{pressed wt. (g)}}{\text{original wt. (g)}} \times 100.$$

PENETROMETER INSTRUCTIONS

The penetrometer (Fig. A.8) is used to objectively evaluate the texture of certain foods. It measures the force required to move a plunger a fixed distance through a food material or it may estimate the distance travelled by a probe when subjected to a given force.

The penetrometer is useful for the following foods:

- Baked custard—use aluminum cone for 30 sec penetration.
- Baked product—use flat plunger for 30 sec penetration.
- Semi-moist confections—needle attachment for 1 min penetration.
- Jellies—use flat plunger for 1 min penetration.
- Vegetables—use needle attachment for 1 min penetration.

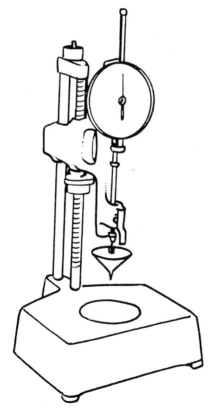

Figure A.8. Universal penetrometer. (From Campbell, A. M., Penfield, M. P., and Griswold, R. M. 1979. *The Experimental Study of Food*, p. 461. Houghton Mifflin, Boston. Reprinted with permission.)

Directions for Use

Preparation

1. Level the machine.
2. Lower the platform.
3. Raise the needle bar.
4. Place the pointer on zero.

Use

1. Place the product on the platform.
2. Contact the food with the attachment—raise the platform first with the large adjustment and then with the small adjustment knobs.
3. While starting the timer, push the level to release the needle bar. Hold for a timed period of penetration.
4. Release the lever to stop the needle bar.
5. Depress the indicator bar for 1/10 mm reading.
6. Record the average of two readings.

LINE SPREAD TEST INSTRUCTIONS

The line spread test is used to measure the consistency of foods in terms of the distance that foods spread on a flat surface in a given period of time. It is suitable for foods such as white sauce, soft custard, applesauce, starch puddings, cake batters, and cream filling.

Equipment for Test

1. A hollow cylinder having a diameter of 5–8 cm. This can be made by removing the handle from a cookie cutter, by cutting both ends out of a small flat tin can, or by cutting heavy copper tubing into cylinders approximately 7 cm high. It also is possible to purchase plumbing fittings that are suitable for line spread rings.
2. Line spread chart*
3. A flat glass plate or a large glass pie plate.
4. A spirit level.

Directions for Use

1. Place the glass plate or pie plate over the chart and check for evenness with the spirit level.

---

*See McWilliams, M. 1981. *Experimental Foods Laboratory Manual*, 2nd ed., p. 175. Plycon Press, Redondo Beach, CA.

2. Place the cylinder directly over the smallest circle and fill with the food to be tested. Level off with a spatula. Remove any food that falls onto the plate. Suspend a thermometer into the test material.
3. When the material reaches the desired temperature, lift the cylinder and allow the food to spread for exactly 1 min.
4. Quickly take readings (at four equally spaced axes) on the limit of spread of the substance.
5. The line spread of the sample is found by averaging the four readings. The value represents the distance in centimeters that the material spreads in 1 min.

pH METER INSTRUCTIONS

The pH Meter

A pH meter is basically a very special voltmeter, with two fundamental requirements. First, it must be capable of accurately measuring small voltage changes at the extremely high impedances exhibited by pH electrodes. Second, it must be adjustable to the pH and voltage characteristics of the electrode system. Modern pH meters fulfill these requirements well, with high-impedance circuitry that draws very little current, and a variety of controls for calibration.

The pH Standard

The pH meter/electrode system is standardized by immersing the electrodes into solutions of known pH value and adjusting the pH meter to display these values. Such solutions are called pH buffer standards. They have the special characteristic of resisting pH change upon dilution or acid/base contamination.

Buffers are available commercially in a variety of forms, including prepared ready-to-use solutions, concentrated solutions, capsules, and prepackaged salts. Each has certain advantages, based on individual storage and use requirements. Figure A.9 lists several buffer solutions that have been established by the National Bureau of Standards, and gives pH values at various temperatures.

For best accuracy, standardization should be performed with a fresh buffer solution whose pH value is close to that of the sample to be tested. In cases where the sample pH is unknown, a two-point standardization is performed. This is done by first standardizing with a buffer whose pH value is close to the zero potential of the electrode system, typically pH 7. The electrodes are then transferred to either an acid or base buffer whose value will most likely bracket the sample pH. The pH value of the second buffer is set on the meter by adjusting the slope control. Buffers should be at the same temperature as the sample for best accuracy.

Active Acid Concentration $[H^+]$		pH		Active Base Concentration $[OH^-]$	
10^0	1.0	0	↑	0.00000000000001	10^{14}
10^1	0.1	1		0.0000000000001	10^{13}
10^2	0.01	2		0.000000000001	10^{12}
10^3	0.001	3		0.00000000001	10^{11}
10^4	0.0001	4		0.0000000001	10^{10}
10^5	0.00001	5	Increasing	0.000000001	10^9
10^6	0.000001	6	Acidity	0.00000001	10^8
10^7	0.0000001	7	Neutrality (Pure Water)	0.0000001	10^7
10^8	0.00000001	8	Increasing	0.000001	10^6
10^9	0.000000001	9	Basicity	0.00001	10^5
10^{10}	0.0000000001	10		0.0001	10^4
10^{11}	0.00000000001	11		0.001	10^3
10^{12}	0.000000000001	12		0.01	10^2
10^{13}	0.0000000000001	13		0.1	10^1
10^{14}	0.00000000000001	14	↓	1.0	10^0

Figure A.9. pH scale. (Courtesy of the Fisher Scientific Co., Pittsburgh, PA.)

User Controls

Before operating the pH meter, locate and become familiar with the function of the front panel controls and the readout display. All are described in detail below and illustrated in Figure A.10.

Front Panel

Function selector. A three-position rotary switch that maintains the instrument on STANDBY (circuitry energized) when measurements are not being taken, and that selects the operating mode (pH for pH determinations and mV for millivolt measurements).

Slope control. A single-turn potentiometer used only in the pH mode to compensate for electrode efficiency. Calibrated over a nominal range of 90–100% of the theoretical slope, the control adjusts amplifier gain to compensate for electrodes that exhibit less than 100% efficient response. When using 100% efficient electrodes, the output of the electrode pair varies at the rate of 59.16 mV per pH unit at 25°C, in accordance with theoretical Nernstian response. In practice, few electrodes exhibit the ideal response; hence the SLOPE control is used to correct the measurement, as required by the particular electrode in use.

Temperature control. A single-turn potentiometer calibrated in 2° increments over the range 0–100°C. This control is used exclusively for manual temperature compensation in the pH-measuring mode. Like the SLOPE control, it adjusts amplifier gain—in this case, to compensate for pH temperature dependence. During operation, it is set initially to the temperature of the standardizing buffer and then to that of each sample.

Standardize control. A multiturn potentiometer that is used in pH determinations to set the meter to the pH value of a buffer solution, thereby compensating for the differences in the zero potential of electrode systems. In millivolt and redox measurements, the control establishes the millivolt zero reference point on the meter.

Readout array. A 4-digit, blue-glow, vacuum fluorescent display having decimal point and minus sign capability; the decimal point is utilized for pH determinations and the minus sign for millivolt measurements. In the pH-measuring mode, test results are displayed over the full 0–14 pH range to the nearest hundredth of a unit and, in the millivolt mode, up to four digits display the results over a range of 0–1999 mV to the nearest 1 mV. The minus sign automatically illuminates when the input millivolt potential is negative. Should the input level exceed the range of the instrument, the right-most three digits are blanked and a 1 or − 1 will be displayed in the left-most digit position. Additionally, when the mode selector is turned to STANDBY, the display is completely blanked except for the decimal point, which remains illuminated as a reminder that the instrument is energized.

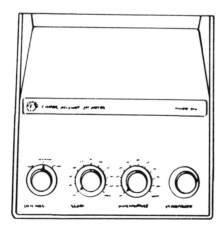

Figure A.10. pH meter-front panel controls. (Courtesy of the Fisher Scientific Co., Pittsburgh, PA.)

Directions for Use

pH Measurements

Prior to making one or a series of pH measurements, the pH meter must be standardized to compensate for the differences in the zero potentials of electrode systems. This requirement is accomplished by immersing the electrode system in a buffer solution of known pH value and adjusting the meter reading to the specified value of the buffer. With this single-point standardization, the slope correction is normally not required for electrodes performing near 100% efficiency and for samples not varying over a range wider than 2 pH units.

In meter standardization, as well as in pH measurements, attention also must be given to the temperatures of both the buffer and the sample solutions because the pH of a solution changes with temperature (buffer pH at a specified temperature is always indicated on the manufacturer's label). Moreover, temperature affects the voltage output of the electrode system. During operation, the latter is generally compensated for by manually adjusting the TEMPERATURE control first to the temperature of the buffer, and then to that of the sample. Optionally, however, the instrument can be equipped with an accessory probe that replaces the TEMPERATURE control in the measuring circuit and provides automatic temperature compensation in the pH-measuring mode.

Note. Proper electrode care is fundamental to obtaining reliable pH measurements. Improper care of electrodes may cause the meter reading to drift, respond slowly, or produce erroneous readings. For this reason, the electrode system should always be conditioned and used in accordance with the separate instructions supplied with each unit. Should there be some doubt whether an erroneous indication is caused by a faulty electrode or by a malfunction of the instrument, refer to the SERVICE section of the pH-unit operating manual.

Using Manual Temperature Compensation

To perform pH measurements using the manual TEMPERATURE control, proceed as follows.

1. Set FUNCTION selector to STANDBY position.
2. Set SLOPE control at 100%.
3. Select a buffer that has a pH value within 1 or 2 units and a temperature within 10°C of the solution to be measured.
4. Immerse electrode system and a thermometer in buffer solution.
   Note: To provide adequate electrolyte flow, make certain that the rubber sleeve has been lowered from over the filling hole of combination or reference electrodes.

5. Wait until electrode system and buffer solution reach thermal equilibrium (thermometer reading steady), then adjust TEMPERATURE control to agree with indicated temperature of buffer solution and record the setting.

   Note. Thermal equilibration period normally requires about 2 min, but varies depending upon temperature difference between electrode system and buffer solution.

6. Determine exact pH of buffer solution from a table of buffer pH versus temperature (usually found on bottle label), and record the value.

7. Set FUNCTION selector to pH position.

8. Adjust STANDARDIZE control until digital display indicates the pH of the buffer solution as determined in step 6.

9. Set FUNCTION selector to STANDBY position.

10. Remove electrode system and thermometer from buffer solution.

11. To avoid contamination of one solution with another, rinse electrode system and thermometer with distilled water before proceeding with pH measurements.

12. Immerse electrode system and a thermometer into sample solution.

13. Wait until electrode system and sample solution reach thermal equilibrium (thermometer reading steady), then adjust TEMPERATURE control to agree with indicated temperature of sample solution.

   Note. Thermal equilibrium normally requires about 2 min, but varies depending upon temperature difference between electrode system and sample solution.

14. Set FUNCTION selector to pH position.

15. Read pH of sample from digital display, and record value. Set FUNCTION selector to STANDBY.

16. Remove electrode system and thermometer from solution.

17. To avoid contamination of one solution with another, rinse electrode system and thermometer with distilled water before proceeding with next measurement.

18. Repeat steps 12–17 for remaining samples that fall within same pH and temperature ranges of the buffer; otherwise, restandardize instrument prior to making measurements by repeating steps 3–17.

19. Following the last measurement, place FUNCTION selector to STANDBY position.

pH and the pH Scale

Since its introduction in 1909, the measurement of pH has become increasingly more important in both laboratory and industrial environments. The close control of pH is of primary importance in life processes; control of acidity is essential in sanitary engineering and electroplating and in the textile, pharmaceutical, and food industries. Modern instrumentation and the availability of a wide variety of electrode styles have made the measurement of pH almost as simple and convenient as the measurement of temperature.

In general, pH is a measure of the degree of acidity or alkalinity of a substance. It is related to the effective or active acid concentration of a solution by the equation

$$pH = -\log a_H, \tag{A.1a}$$

with a_H representing the activity of the hydrogen ions in the solution. Neglecting activity effects, Eq. (A.1a) reduces to

$$pH = -\log [H^+], \tag{A.1b}$$

with $[H^+]$ representing the concentration of the hydrogen ions in the solution. pH is sometimes referred to as the power of the hydrogen ion in solution. Thus, the pH of the strong acid 0.01 molar HCl is equal to 2, because the hydrogen ion concentration is 10^2 molar:

$$pH = -\log [10^2] = 2.$$

The pH scale usually ranges from 0 to 14, or from an active acid concentration of $[1 \times 10^0]$ to $[1 \times 10^{14}]$ (1.0 molar to 0.00000000000001 molar). Although acid concentrations outside this range can and do exist, they are not generally encountered in practice.

The pH scale is based on the dissociation constant of water. In pure water, a very small number of molecules react with one another to form hydronium ions (H_3O^+)—which account for acidic properties—and hydroxide ions (OH^-)—which account for the basic properties of an aqueous solution:

$$2H_2O \rightleftharpoons H_3O^+ + OH^- \tag{A.2}$$

or, for simplicity,

$$H_2O \rightleftharpoons H^+ + OH^-. \tag{A.3}$$

At 25°C, pure water dissociates until the acid $[H^+]$ and base $[OH^-]$ concentrations are equal, at 1×10^7 molar. The product of both concentrations is the dissociation constant K_w:

$$K_w = [H^+]\,[OH^-]$$
$$= [1 \times 10^7]\,[1 \times 10^7]$$
$$= [1 \times 10^{14}]. \tag{A.4}$$

Because the hydronium ion concentration $[H^+]$ equals 1×10^7, the pH of pure water at 25°C is 7. This is referred to as the neutrality point. In aqueous solutions, at 25°C, the product of $[H^+]$ and $[OH^-]$ must always remain constant at 1×10^{14}. Therefore, an increase in either the acid or base concentration will always result in a decrease in the other term. Hence, a solution of the strong base 0.01 M NaOH will have a hydrogen-ion concentration of

$$H^+ = \frac{K_w}{[OH^-]} = \frac{10^{14}}{10^2} = 10^{12},$$

and from Eq. (A.1),

$$pH = -\log [10^{12}] = 12.$$

POTENTIOMETRIC MEASUREMENT OF pH

The pH value of a sample can be determined using colorimetric indicator solutions or indicator papers. However, the preferred method is performed potentiometrically, using a pH meter and electrode system.

This method is based on the fact that, when certain electrodes are immersed in a solution, a voltage is produced that is related in a very precise way to the pH of the solution. This voltage can be predicted by the Nernst equation. In simplified form, the equation is

$$E = E_0 \frac{-2.303}{F} RT\,(\text{pH}),$$

where E is the measured voltage, E_0 is the total of all constant voltages in the measuring system, R is the Gas Law constant, T is the temperature in °K, and F is Faraday's constant.

The measuring system is composed of the following.

1. Two electrodes—a glass indicating electrode, which develops a potential dependent on the pH of a solution, and a reference electrode, which provides a constant potential and completes the electrical circuit.
2. A pH meter or electrometer—a device capable of measuring small potential differences in a circuit of extremely high resistance.

3. One or more standard solutions of known pH values for proper standardization of the system.

Electrodes

The Glass Indicating Electrode
The pH-sensing electrode—usually called simply a "glass electrode"—is contained in a nonconducting glass tube, called the body. This is sealed to a bulb of special conductive glass, the pH-sensing membrane. The body is filled with a buffered electrolyte whose pH value and ionic concentration are fixed. An internal reference element, typically Ag/AgCl, is immersed in this filling solution. This design assures that constant potentials are developed on the inner surface of the glass membrane, and on the internal reference element. When the electrode is immersed in a solution of pH 7, the sum of these fixed voltages approximately balances the voltage developed on the outer surface of the glass membrane and the separate reference electrode. Thus, the total potential output of the system is near 0 mV. In solutions of more or less than pH 7, the potential on the outer membrane surface changes in proportion to the sample pH. The voltage change is sensed by the meter and displayed as a pH value (see Fig. A.11).

The Reference Electrode
One major requirement of the reference electrode is to complete the electrical measuring circuit. A simple wire, immersed in the sample solution, could satisfy this purpose. But this simplified arrangement would be susceptible to voltage changes, dependent on the time in the solution and the sample composition. Such voltage changes would be unacceptable, of course, because the second (and most important) requirement of a reference electrode is to provide a stable reference potential. Hence, a reference ele-

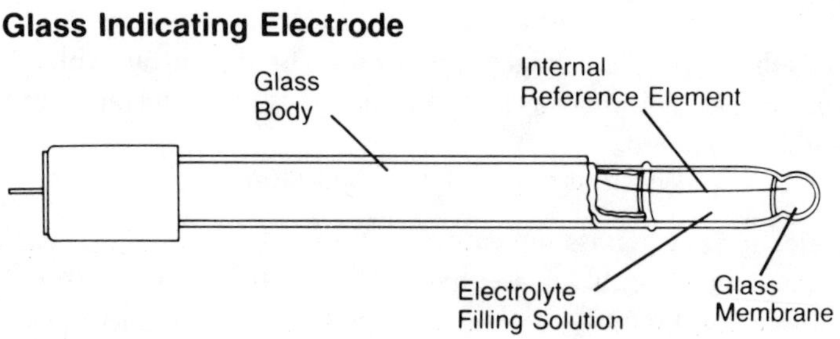

Glass Indicating Electrode

Figure A.11. Glass indicating electrode. (Courtesy of the Fisher Scientific Co., Pittsburgh, PA.)

Reference Electrode

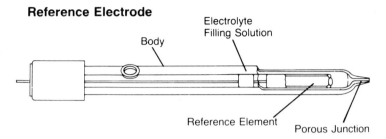

Figure A.12. Reference electrode. (Courtesy of the Fisher Scientific Co., Pittsburgh, PA.)

ment, usually calomel or silver/silver chloride, is immersed in an electrolyte filling solution of fixed ionic concentration, contained in the probe body. This produces the required constant voltage, no matter what the sample composition. The electrical circuit is completed by allowing a small flow of the electrolyte to pass through a porous junction in the probe tip (Fig. A.12).

Appendix B

Essentials of the Metric System

PREFIXES AND BASE UNITS

Prefixes

To operate within the metric system, it is necessary to know the prefixes used within the system and their meanings. The following presentation includes a number of prefixes that might be encountered occasionally, but it is probable that kilo, centi, and milli are the ones that will be utilized extensively in food experimentation.

tera	T	$10^{12} = 1,000,000,000,000$
giga	G	$10^{9} = 1,000,000,000$
mega	M	$10^{6} = 1,000,000$
kilo	k	$10^{3} = 1000$
hecto	h	$10^{2} = 100$
deka	da	$10^{1} = 10$
		$10^{0} = 1$
deci	d	$10^{-1} = 0.1$
centi	c	$10^{-2} = 0.01$
milli	m	$10^{-3} = 0.001$
micro	μ	$10^{-6} = 0.000001$
nano	n	$10^{-9} = 0.000000001$

Base Units and Equivalencies

Mass

pound	453.6 grams
ounce	28.35 grams
kilogram	2.2 pounds

184

Volume

quart	0.946 liter
cup	236.6 milliliters
tablespoon	14.79 milliliters
teaspoon	4.93 milliliters
fluid ounce	29.57 milliliters
quart	1.057 quarts

Length

inch	2.54 centimeters
yard	0.914 meter
meter	39.37 inches

SOURCE: McWilliams, M. 1981. *Experimental Foods Laboratory Manual*, p. 174. Plycon Press, Redondo Beach, CA. Reprinted with permission.

Table B.1. Table of Equivalents

ABBREVIATIONS AND SYMBOLS		WEIGHT AND VOLUME EQUIVALENTS
Capacity	*Temperature*	*Common Units of Weight*
Bushel (bu)	Degrees Centigrade (°C)	1 gram = 0.035 ounces
Cubic Centimeter (cc)	Degrees Fahrenheit (°F)	1 kilogram = 2.21 pounds
Cup (c)		1 ounce = 28.35 grams
Fluid ounce (fl oz)	*Length*	1 pound = 453.59 grams
Gallon (gal)	Centimeter (cm)	
Gill (gil)	Foot (ft)	*Common Units of Volume*
Liter (l)	Inch (in)	1 bushel = 4 pecks
Milliliter (ml)	Meter (m)	1 peck = 8 quarts
Pint (pt)	Millimeter (mm)	1 gallon = 4 quarts
Quart (qt)	Millimicron (mμ)	1 quart = 2 pints
Peck (pk)		= 946.4 milliliters
Tablespoon (Tbsp)	*Weight*	1 pint = 2 cups
Teaspoon (tsp)	Gram (g)	1 cup = 16 tablespoons
	Kilogram (kg)	= 2 gills
Time	Microgram (mcg) or (μg)	= 8 fluid ounces
Hour (hr)	Milligram (mg)	= 236.6 milliliters
Minute (min)	Ounce (oz)	1 tablespoon = 3 teaspoons
Second (sec)	Pound (lb)	= 1/2 fluid ounce
		= 14.8 milliliters
		1 teaspoon = 4.9 milliliters
		1 liter = 1000 milliliters
		= 1.06 quarts

SOURCE: American Home Economics Association. 1980. *Handbook of Food Preparation*, p. 25. Author, Washington, D.C. Reprinted with permission.

Table B.2. Equivalents for one Unit and Fractions of a Unit

Tablespoon	Cup	Pint
1 Tbsp = 3 tsp	1 c = 16 Tbsp	1 pt = 2 c
$7/8$ Tbsp = $2^{1}/_{2}$ tsp	$7/8$ c = 14 Tbsp	$7/8$ pt = $1^{3}/_{4}$ c
$3/4$ Tbsp = $2^{1}/_{4}$ tsp	$3/4$ c = 12 Tbsp	$3/4$ pt = $1^{1}/_{2}$ c
$2/3$ Tbsp = 2 tsp	$2/3$ c = $10^{2}/_{3}$ Tbsp	$2/3$ pt = $1^{1}/_{3}$ c
$5/8$ Tbsp = $1^{7}/_{8}$ tsp	$5/8$ c = 10 Tbsp	$5/8$ pt = $1^{1}/_{4}$ c
$1/2$ Tbsp = $1^{1}/_{2}$ tsp	$1/2$ c = 8 Tbsp	$1/2$ pt = 1 c
$3/8$ Tbsp = $1^{1}/_{8}$ tsp	$3/8$ c = 6 Tbsp	$3/8$ pt = $3/4$ c
$1/3$ Tbsp = 1 tsp	$1/3$ c = $5^{1}/_{3}$ Tbsp	$1/3$ pt = $2/3$ c
$1/4$ Tbsp = $3/4$ tsp	$1/4$ c = 4 Tbsp	$1/4$ pt = $1/2$ c
	$1/8$ c = 2 Tbsp	$1/8$ pt = $1/4$ c
Quart	$1/16$ c = 1 Tbsp	$1/16$ pt = 2 Tbsp
1 qt = 2 pt		
$7/8$ qt = $3^{1}/_{2}$ c	*Gallon*	*Pound*
$3/4$ qt = 3 c	1 gal = 4 qt	1 lb = 16 oz
$2/3$ qt = $2^{2}/_{3}$ c	$7/8$ gal = $3^{1}/_{2}$ qt	$7/8$ lb = 14 oz
$5/8$ qt = $2^{1}/_{2}$ c	$3/4$ gal = 3 qt	$3/4$ lb = 12 oz
$1/2$ qt = 1 pt	$2/3$ gal = $10^{2}/_{3}$ c	$2/3$ lb = $10^{2}/_{3}$ oz
$3/8$ qt = $1^{1}/_{2}$ c	$5/8$ gal = 5 pt	$5/8$ lb = 10 oz
$1/3$ qt = $1^{1}/_{3}$ c	$1/2$ gal = 2 qt	$1/2$ lb = 8 oz
$1/4$ qt = 1 c	$3/8$ gal = 3 pt	$3/8$ lb = 6 oz
$1/8$ qt = $1/2$ c	$1/3$ gal = $5^{1}/_{3}$ c	$1/3$ lb = $5^{1}/_{3}$ oz
$1/16$ qt = $1/4$ c	$1/4$ gal = 1 qt	$1/4$ lb = 4 oz
	$1/8$ gal = 1 pt	$1/8$ lb = 2 oz
	$1/16$ gal = 1 c	$1/16$ lb = 1 oz

SOURCE: American Home Economics Association. 1980. *Handbook of Food Preparation*, p. 25. Author, Washington, D.C. Reprinted with permission.

Table B.3. Conversion to Metric Units

Comparison of Avoirdupois and Metric Units of Weight

oz	g	lb	kg	g	oz	kg	lb
1 = 0.06 lb =	28.35	1 = 0.454		1 = 0.035		1 =	2.205
2 = 0.12 lb =	56.70	2 = 0.91		2 = 0.07		2 =	4.41
3 = 0.19 lb =	85.05	3 = 1.36		3 = 0.11		3 =	6.61
4 = 0.25 lb =	113.40	4 = 1.81		4 = 0.14		4 =	8.82
5 = 0.31 lb =	141.75	5 = 2.27		5 = 0.18		5 =	11.02
6 = 0.38 lb =	170.10	6 = 2.72		6 = 0.21		6 =	13.23
7 = 0.44 lb =	198.45	7 = 3.18		7 = 0.25		7 =	15.43
8 = 0.50 lb =	226.80	8 = 3.63		8 = 0.28		8 =	17.64
9 = 0.56 lb =	255.15	9 = 4.08		9 = 0.32		9 =	19.84
10 = 0.62 lb =	283.50	10 = 4.54		10 = 0.35		10 =	22.05
11 = 0.69 lb =	311.85	11 = 4.99		11 = 0.39		11 =	24.26
12 = 0.75 lb =	340.20	12 = 5.44		12 = 0.42		12 =	26.46
13 = 0.81 lb =	368.55	13 = 5.90		13 = 0.46		13 =	28.67
14 = 0.88 lb =	396.90	14 = 6.35		14 = 0.49		14 =	30.87
15 = 0.94 lb =	425.25	15 = 6.81		15 = 0.53		15 =	33.08
16 = 1.00 lb =	453.59	16 = 7.26		16 = 0.56		16 =	35.28

Comparison of U.S. and Metric Units of Liquid Measure

fl oz	ml	qt	L	gal	L	ml	fl oz	L	qt	L	gal
1 =	29.573	1 = 0.946		1 =	3.785	1 = 0.034		1 =	1.057	1 = 0.264	
2 =	59.15	2 = 1.89		2 =	7.57	2 = 0.07		2 =	2.11	2 = 0.53	
3 =	88.72	3 = 2.84		3 =	11.36	3 = 0.10		3 =	3.17	3 = 0.79	
4 =	118.30	4 = 3.79		4 =	15.14	4 = 0.14		4 =	4.23	4 = 1.06	
5 =	147.87	5 = 4.73		5 =	18.93	5 = 0.17		5 =	5.28	5 = 1.32	
6 =	177.44	6 = 5.68		6 =	22.71	6 = 0.20		6 =	6.34	6 = 1.59	
7 =	207.02	7 = 6.62		7 =	26.50	7 = 0.24		7 =	7.40	7 = 1.85	
8 =	236.59	8 = 7.57		8 =	30.28	8 = 0.27		8 =	8.45	8 = 2.11	
9 =	266.16	9 = 8.52		9 =	34.07	9 = 0.30		9 =	9.51	9 = 2.38	
10 =	295.73	10 = 9.46		10 =	37.85	10 = 0.34		10 =	10.57	10 = 2.64	

SOURCE: American Home Economics Association. 1980. *Handbook of Food Preparation*, p. 26. Author, Washington, D.C. Reprinted with permission.

Table B.4. Temperature Conversion Table (Degrees Centigrade to Fahrenheit)

DEGREES

Centigrade	0	1	2	3	4	5	6	7	8	9
−2	−4°F	−6°	−8°	−9°	−11°	−13°	−15°	−17°	−18°	−20°
−1	14°	12°	10°	9°	7°	5°	3°	1°	0°	−2°
−0	32°	30°	28°	27°	25°	23°	21°	19°	18°	16°
0	32°	34°	36°	37°	39°	41°	43°	45°	46°	48°
1	50°	52°	54°	55°	57°	59°	61°	63°	64°	66°
2	68°	70°	72°	73°	75°	77°	79°	81°	82°	84°
3	86°	88°	90°	91°	93°	95°	97°	99°	100°	102°
4	104°	106°	108°	109°	111°	113°	115°	117°	118°	120°
5	122°	124°	126°	127°	129°	131°	133°	135°	136°	138°
6	140°	142°	144°	145°	147°	149°	151°	153°	154°	156°
7	158°	160°	162°	163°	165°	167°	169°	171°	172°	174°
8	176°	178°	180°	181°	183°	185°	187°	189°	190°	192°
9	194°	196°	198°	199°	201°	203°	205°	207°	208°	210°
10	212°	214°	216°	217°	219°	221°	223°	225°	226°	228°
11	230°	232°	234°	235°	237°	239°	241°	243°	244°	246°
12	248°	250°	252°	253°	255°	257°	259°	261°	262°	264°
13	266°	268°	270°	271°	273°	275°	277°	279°	280°	282°
14	284°	286°	288°	289°	291°	293°	295°	297°	298°	300°
15	302°	304°	306°	307°	309°	311°	313°	315°	316°	318°
16	320°	322°	324°	325°	327°	329°	331°	333°	334°	336°
17	338°	340°	342°	343°	345°	347°	349°	351°	352°	354°
18	356°	358°	360°	361°	363°	365°	367°	369°	370°	372°
19	374°	376°	378°	379°	381°	383°	385°	387°	388°	390°
20	392°	394°	396°	397°	399°	401°	403°	405°	406°	408°
21	410°	412°	414°	415°	417°	419°	421°	423°	424°	426°
22	428°	430°	432°	433°	435°	437°	439°	441°	442°	444°

(continued)

Table B.4. (*Continued*)

DEGREES

Centigrade	0	1	2	3	4	5	6	7	8	9
23	446°	448°	450°	451°	453°	455°	457°	459°	460°	462°
24	464°	466°	468°	469°	471°	473°	475°	477°	478°	480°
25	482°	484°	486°	487°	489°	491°	493°	495°	496°	498°
26	500°	502°	504°	505°	507°	509°	511°	513°	514°	516°
27	518°	520°	522°	523°	525°	527°	529°	531°	532°	534°
28	536°	538°	540°	541°	543°	545°	547°	549°	550°	552°
29	554°	556°	558°	559°	561°	563°	565°	567°	568°	570°
30	572°	574°	576°	577°	579°	581°	583°	585°	586°	588°

NOTE: The numbers in the body of the table give in degrees Fahrenheit the temperature indicated in degrees Centigrade at the top and side. To convert 178°C to the Fahrenheit scale, find 17 in the column headed degrees C. Proceed in a horizontal line to the column headed 8, which shows 352°F as corresponding to 178°C. To convert 352°F to the Celsius (centigrade) scale, find 352 in the Fahrenheit readings, then in the column headed degrees C, find the number that is on the same horizontal line, i.e., 17. Next, fill in the last number from the heading of the column in which 352 was found, i.e., 8, resulting in 178°C, which is equivalent to 352°F.
Range: −29°C (−20°F) to 309°C (588°F).

Conversion formula: $T(°C) = 5/9 \ (T(°F) - 32); \ T(°F) = 9/5 \ T(°C) + 32.$

SOURCE: American Home Economics Association. 1980. *Handbook of Food Preparation*, pp. 20–21. Author, Washington, D.C. Reprinted with permission.

Appendix C

Average Weights of Selected Foods

Table A.5. Average Weight of a Measured Cup of Selected Foods

FOOD	FORM	WEIGHT (g/cup)	FOOD	FORM	WEIGHT (g/cup)
Almonds	Blanched		Bulgur	Uncooked	140
	whole	157	Cheese		
	chopped	127	cheddar	Shredded	98
Apples	Raw, pared		cottage	Creamed	233
	chopped	124	cream		230
	diced	109	mozzarella	Chopped	112
	quartered	122	Swiss	Shredded	108
	sliced	108	Chicken	Cooked, deboned	144
	Cooked		Chocolate	Chips	167
	slices,		Cocoa		86
	no sugar	207	Cocoa mix		139
Baking	Double		Coconut	Fresh, grated	80
powder	acting	177		Dehydrated	
Barley	Uncooked	195		flakes	88
Beans				shredded	91
black	Uncooked	184	Coffee	Freeze-dried	60
Great	Dry,		Cookies		
northern	uncooked	178	ginger-		
green	Uncooked,		snaps	Crumbs	115
	fresh	107	vanilla		
Mung	Dry,		wafers	Crumbs	104
	uncooked	203	Corn grits	Uncooked	162
Pea	Dry,		Cornmeal		
	uncooked	199	white	Uncooked	140
Soy	Dry,		yellow	Uncooked	151
	uncooked	173	Corn syrup		325
	Curd,		Crackers		
	1/2 in. cubes	184	Graham	Crumbs	84
Beef	Ground,		snack	Crumbs	80
	uncooked	226	Cream	Sour	242
Bread	Crumbs, dry	107		Whipping	232
	soft	43	Currants	Dehydrated	131
Bread	Cubes, dry	42	Dates	Dehydrated,	
	soft	40		pitted, chopped	171

(continued)

FOOD	FORM	WEIGHT (g/cup)	FOOD	FORM	WEIGHT (g/cup)
Eggs	Whites	255	Rice		
	Whole	251	brown	Long grain, raw	176
	Yolks	240		Short grain, raw	194
Flour			white	Long grain, raw	192
barley	Unsifted, spooned	102		Medium grain, raw	194
oat	Coarse, unsifted	120		Short grain, raw	200
	Fine, unsifted	96		Parboiled, raw	181
potato	Unsifted, spooned	179	Sugar	Brown, packed	211
rice	Brown, unsifted	158		Brownulated	152
	White, unsifted	149		Confectioner's	
rye	Dark, stirred	127		unsifted	113
	Light, unsifted	101		sifted	95
	Whole grain,			Granulated	196
	unsifted	82		Raw	195
soy	Full-fat, unsifted	96		Superfine	197
tapioca	Unsifted	120	Sunflower	Seeds, hulled	125
Gelatin	Flavored	187	Tapioca	Quick-cooking	160
Honey	Strained	325	Walnuts	English, chopped	120
Lemon	Juice	223	Wheat	All-purpose	
Lemons	Fresh juice	250		unsifted	
Lentils	Dry, uncooked	186		spooned	126
Macaroni	Elbow, uncooked	130		dipped	143
Margarine	Regular	225		sifted	
	Soft	208		spooned	116
Mayonnaise	Regular	240		Bread	
	Low-calorie	244		unsifted	
Milk	Fresh, fluid			spooned	123
	whole	241		dipped	136
	skim	246		sifted	
	Nonfat, dry			spooned	117
	instant	74		Cake	
	spray	134		unsifted	
Molasses		309		spooned	111
Mustard	Prepared	251		dipped	119
Noodles	Uncooked, medium	38		sifted	
	Uncooked, thin	45		spooned	99
Oats	Quick, uncooked	73		Germ, spooned	115
rolled	Regular, uncooked	75		Gluten	
Oil	Cooking	209		unsifted	
Onions,	Uncooked			spooned	135
dry	chopped	171		dipped	142
	grated	231		sifted	
	ground	238		spooned	136
	slices	113		Self-rising	
Parsley	Dried, flakes	15		unsifted	
Peanut	Crunchy	261		spooned	127
butter	Smooth	251		dipped	130
Peanuts	Salted, chopped	138		sifted	
Pecans,	Chopped	108		spooned	106
shelled	Halves	108		Starch, unsifted,	
Potatoes	Fresh, raw, diced	161		spooned	123
	Dry flakes	55		Whole wheat	
	Dry granules	201		stirred,	
Raisins	Uncooked, whole	144		spooned	120

FOOD	FORM	WEIGHT (g/cup)	FOOD	FORM	WEIGHT (g/cup)
Whey	Liquid	244		Whole milk,	
Yeast	Active dry	142		partially	
Yogurt	Whole milk	245		skimmed	249

SOURCE: McWilliams, M. 1981. *Experimental Foods Laboratory Manual*, 2nd ed., p. 178. Plycon Press, Redondo Beach, CA. Reprinted with permission.

General Subject Index

About the Author

Dana B. Ott, Ph.D., R.D., is an assistant professor of food science in the Department of Food Science and Human Nutrition at Michigan State University. Dr. Ott has traveled the United States while acquiring her education, receiving a B.S. degree in Foods and Nutrition at California State Polytechnic University, an M.S. degree in Foods and Nutrition at the University of Nebraska, and a Ph.D. degree in Food Science at Rutgers University in 1982. Dr. Ott is also a registered dietitian and completed her dietetic internship at the University of Nebraska. After receiving her degree, Dr. Ott taught human nutrition at Texas A & M University in the Department of Animal Science until July of 1984. She then joined the Michigan State University faculty. Dr. Ott is the author of several scientific articles concerning food science and nutrition and is a member of many professional organizations, including the Institute of Food Technologists, American Institute of Nutrition, and the American Dietetic Association.

Dr. Ott has received numerous academic awards and has been recognized on numerous occasions by her students at Michigan State University for excellence in teaching. In 1986, Michigan State University presented Dr. Ott with the Teacher–Scholar Award. Dr. Ott teaches an experimental foods course and a course on consumer trends in the food industry. Her major research area focuses on nutrient retention during processing and storage of foods.

DATE DUE